DORSET
DIALECT DAYS

James Attwell

Shillingstone

dpc

DORSET PUBLISHING COMPANY
KNOCK-NA-CRE, MILBORNE PORT
SHERBORNE, DORSET DT9 5HJ

Publishing details. First published 1987.
Copyright James Attwell © 1987.
Restrictions upon copying. All rights reserved. No
part of this publication may be reproduced, stored in a
retrieval system, or transmitted in any form or by any
means, electronic, computerised, mechanical,
photocopying, recording or otherwise, without prior
permission in writing from the publishers.
Printed in Great Britain by Wincanton Litho, at the
Old National School, North Street, Wincanton,
Somerset, telephone (0963) 33643.
Typeset by Irene Howard at SOS, 1 Bell Street,
Shaftesbury, Dorset.
International standard book number
[ISBN] 0 902129 91 0

How I remember bread and cheese –
　The make-believe on hawthorn trees –
And later tasting hips and haws
　Against the rules and bird-land laws.
Confessed addiction to the taste
　Of bitter sorrel in the waste
Of fields content with cows all day,
　Who chewed – and sometimes looked my way.
The apples offered, taken free,
　And sweeter ones – illegally.
A sweeter draught than anything
　The hand-cupped water from the spring;
Do modern little faces press
　Against the coolest water cress;
But would eyes gaze with some disdain,
　If I came back to taste again?

My poem, first published in *The Dorset Year Book,* led to my writing this book.
All the events and characters are factual, but, with a few exceptions, only
members of my family are named.

On top of Cranborne Chase

Stalbridge

Dorset woods and downs

1

STUDENTS OF the dialect should acquire the *Grammar and Glossary of the Dorset Dialect, with the History, Outspreading and Bearings of South-Western English* compiled by William Barnes. The first edition was published in Berlin in 1863. I have attempted to record some of the dialect in use during the nineteen thirties and beyond, some seventy years after the William Barnes Glossary was published.

Thomas Hardy recorded that much of the dialect had been lost since William Barnes's day and it will be seen that much more has been lost since Thomas Hardy wrote his tribute to William Barnes. I have recorded all the words within my memory, many of which were used by my family. It is interesting to note that my grandmother lived only a mile from Barnes's house and would have used much of his dialect, yet, at her knee, some fifty years later, I found only about one in ten of those words were in use.

I have tried to record some of the abbreviations within the dialect and some of the oddities which occur, especially in the rural areas.

I quote William Barnes for "the main sounds":

1. *ee* as in beet
2. *e* as in Dorset [a sound between 1 and 3]
3. *a* as in mate
4. *i* as in birth
5. *a* as in father
6. *aw* as in awe
7. *o* as in dote
8. *oo* as in rood

To this I would add:

9. *oo* as in foot [voot] comes near to the *u* sound as in put
10. *e* or *i* before *r* producing the Dorset *burr* as in merge, dirge, verge [purse the lips to whistle, then say the word birth, as in 4]

In recent times we have been made aware of the American accent and a study of the Dorset dialect will show from which part of the globe much American English originated. Fall or vall [autumn] is a good example. The *tt* sound, is often changed in the dialect to the *dd* sound, i.e. bedder [better] madder [matter] and adder. for, atter [after]. This also occurs in the single *t* as in git [get] which in Dorset can be gid; a word common to the New World and to other dialects in this country. This is a basic glossary, with *sounds* being shown in *italics* and **dialect words** or **expressions** in **bold** type:

a In the dialect almost any verb may have *a*- before it, a-ploughen, a-zowen and so on
a at times replaces *e* before *g* as in agg [egg], bag [beg], lag [leg], pag [peg]
a in the broader accent often becomes *u* as vur [far]
a often preceded by an additional *e,* changing *ā* to *ä* as in feäce [face]

acker = pal, mate, friend
a-dreven = driven
ah = yes [for emphasis: ooh ah, oh yes]

aller = the alder tree
apiece = for each
a'r'n = e'er a one
as how = that ["**I thought as how I could**"]
a's'n = ask him
a-stooded = with wheels stuck fast in soft soil
ate = eat [in broader accent used as present tense, "**come an' ate yur tae**"]
a-thirt = athwart, across
atter = after [at times adder]
a-vore = afore, before
a-vrighted = frightened
ax = ask

back-along = time past
back'ards = backwards
bäde = bed
baff = bath
bag = beg
barried = borrowed
barton = cattle yard
baub = bulb
be = is [or sometimes by]
beänt = be not
best = excel [get the better of]
bile = boil
bin = been
bisom = besom [or a somewhat naughty person]
bissen = be not
bist = be you
bithywin' [withwind] = convolvulus, or bindweed
bittle = beetle [at times biddle] also hammer
bleäre = blare, low as a cow
brack = breach
braed = bread
breadf = breadth
brick = break [of a perfect item: "**nar' brick nor brack**"]
broff = broth
brush or **broush** = brushwood, small branches or twigs of tree
builded = as past tense, "**the bird builded its nest**"
bŭrry = berry or bury
bust = burst
bwoäts = boats or boots
bwoth = both
bwoy = boy

can't = cannot, sometimes pronounced as '**kaint**' as in 'saint'
car = carry
carse = course
ca's = canst
cassen = canst not, can't [An endearing remark I heard passed of a friend who

catched = caught [he were catched]

ceäke = cake

charlick = charlock or field mustard – a common weed

chimley = chimney

chuck = to throw underhand

churry = cherry

claps = clasp

click = clique

close = clothes

clout = hit, or item of clothing

come to pass = old English for happen or occur

conkers = fruit of horse chestnut [though earlier hip of the brier]

'cos = because [now common to modern English]

cou'den = could not

cou's = couldst

coussen = couldst not, could you not

creepen jinnies = wood lice

croop, or croopy down = bend down low

crope = crept

'cross = across

curlywigs = earwigs

cuss = curse

cutty wren = kittywren

cwoin = coin

d sometimes used for *th* as in drash [thrash] dread [thread] drush [thrush]

d' = do. Improves flow of dialect in rural conversation, though *do* for emphasis. ie: "**I d' think an' I d' wonder, but I *do* know**"

dare-say = expect so

dares-n [or dares-n't] = dares not

dench = quench, as fire

dewberry = blackberry [a larger variety]

did [or do] = additional, as in old English. "I do go./I did go"

didden = did not

diddies = gipsies

dissen = didst not, did not

disn't = didst not, did not

di'st = didst, did

'doman = old woman

doos't = dost thou, do you

dosn't = does not, do not

drash = thrash, thresh

dread = thread

dreaten = threaten

dree = three

drillen = drilling "**It do want a drillen**" [it is difficult]

drough = through

drove = though this is a herd or flock in motion, in the dialect it can be the place where they are driven by the drover. ie. a lane

drow = throw

drug = brake for wagon

druppence = three pence

drush = thrush

dunch = wood fire, burning badly

dwon't = don't

dwon't knoow = don't know. Not to be confused with the mid-Atlantic *dunno* which is used by many leading figures in the 1980s. The age of bad speech?

ea = from the sound of *ee* as in reach, the *a* becomes *ä*. A great number of words are affected, ie: peäch, reäch, teäch and so on. Many *ai* spellings change to *ea*. main [meän], rain [reän], again [ageän]

'ee = ye, thee, you

eet = yet. ie: **eet vur all.** [yet vor all] – yet for all that

elem = elm

'em = them, they

emmet = ant

en = in place of *ing*. **ringen** [ringing] not the lazy ringin'. It may be noted that from the nineteen sixties it is commonplace to lose the *g* of *ing*. Even those responsible for education and speakers throughout the land talk in the *comin' and goin'* manner. The sound of the Dorset *en* should not be confused with the modern lazy speech.

evet = eft

f is often interchangeable with *v*. On finding [vinden] a word beginning with *v* use *f* which may reveal the word.

fall [or vall] = autumn [vall more common for "fall down"]

feäce or veäče = face

flag = a water plant, the wild iris

flushed = fledged **"flushed and flew"** fledged and flown

for'ward = forward

fowsty = fusty

'front = afront

gander = look

gap = gape

gearden = garden

gi'd = gave

gi'me = give me

gi'us = give me [not us] **"I'm gwoen zhoppen, zoo gi'us zome money"**

git = get [often **gid,** as other dialects and the American English]

gilcup = buttercup

girt = great [to emphasize, girt big]

goo = go

grab = grapple or grapnel [as from river]

granfer = grandfather

greäte = grate

groun' = ground
gwoad = goad
gwoen [or gooen] = going
gwoold = gold

hackle = work. The hackles [cock's comb] must rise before the fight, or it won't work. Thus, hackle: work
hadden = had not
hado'm = had of them [had hold of]
handy = near
han't = haven't
haps = hasp
har' = harrow
har'ble = horrible
hassen = hast not
hauck = cough
haulm = stalks of plants, as potatoes
hawk = shout
he = it
heal = cover
he'm = he am [is]
het = heat, or to hit [for heat, often **heät**]
he've = he have [has]
hid = head
hidge = hedge
hile = stack of corn sheaves, stood to dry [also oil]
hiszelf = himself
hook = gore, as a horned animal
holler = hollow, vale, or to shout
hook off = direction to horse
hoss = horse
how do = how do you do
how't = how art, or how bist [how are you, or how be you]
hunderd = hundred

I = in the broader sense used as *me* **[not vur I, thank 'ee]**
idden [or idd'n] = is not
inta = into

jay = joy
jine = join
jist = just

kag = keg
kiddle = kettle
knap = hillock, knob, knob-like bud [in knap, in bud]

lack [or lo'k] = look [often lack see, you see]
lacs = lots – of money [from Anglo–Indian – a post 17th century import – the

Hindustani **lakh,** meaning one thousand. A lakh of rupees was worth £10,000

laggens = leggings
lags = legs
langth = length
'lascit = elastic
lats = laths
leän = lean
leäne = lane
'leb'm = eleven
leer [or leery] = empty, or hungry
lew = shelter from cold wind
'llow = allow, reckon
'lotment = allotment
lowl = loll
lummick = stupid person

mammet [or mommet] = image, scarecrow, unsightly person
mar' = marrow [vegetable marrow]
marnen 'ood = morning wood [kindling wood]
meäde = made or mead [meadow]
medder = meadow
me = my [often used together, **"I got my spade, but not me hoe"**]
'member = remember
mid = might
midden = might not
mighty = great, very
min' = mind, mind you, you must know, understand
mit = meet
moot = stump and root of felled tree
more = root of plant or part
mud'n [or mussen] = mustn't
muggy = warm damp weather
murry = merry
mussen [or must'n] = must not

n often follows a word. A simple form big-n [big woone, big one]. Another example is, told him, which should be twold'm, but becomes twold'n.

'namel = enamel
nar'n = never a one [sometimes **nar'**]
need'n = need not
need'm = need them
ne'r = near
nésh = soft, tender, as a plant's growth
never = broadly for 'did not' **[no, she never]**
nevew = nephew
nise = noise
nitch = bundle of wood, for kindling

noo = no [no often means not] **"Whether she did or noo"**

'nother = another or other [**zummit or 'nother** – something or other]

nurly = nearly

nŭss = nurse

nwone = not one. Broadly double negative often used. **"Han't got none"** [have none]

o often becomes *a* in the more rural areas [sound 5] ie: **martal**, mortal. **marn**, morn. A greeting may be: **'marnen** [good is lost] *o* is often *oo* as in rood. **Noo**, no. **Goo**, go. *o* at times *u* as **fur**, for. It will be seen that *o* is often preceded by *w*. Almost any word containing an *o* with sound 7, can have the additional *w* before it. Thus by reading the word without the *w* might reveal the standard word: **woak, bwold, cwold, mwold, swold, twold.** The dialect sound of *ow* in the following words is best shown thus: **héow néow bréown céow,** as opposed to "haow naow braown caow"

o' = of [of often used as on, **"if you come of a Sunday"**]

o'm = of them

o'n = of him

'ood = wood [strangely, the *w* is lost]

ooh = oh. Used to emphasize, as in **"ooh ah** [yes]"

'ool = wool

or'nary = ordinary, plain, even ugly

o's = of us

ou = often sounds as *au* ie: aught [ought]

pāes = peas

pags = pegs

palm = pussy willow

palmer = caterpillar

passon = parson [for reader's amusement I record a remark of my father: **"I passed Passon down ztreet an' didden knoow 'twere Passon till I'd a-pass'n"**]

peäce = peace or piece [broader, **pi'ce**]

peärt = pert

peewit = lapwing

peff = very soft or rotten wood

penn'eth = pennyworth

per'aps = perhaps

perty [or perdy] = pretty

pianer = piano

pinches = stomach-ache

pitch = to put up hay

plim = to swell out

ply = to bend

'po'me-zam [or 'po'me-zoul] = upon my soul

pook = large heap of drying hay

posh = much money. That which the posh [smart set] have

8

pre'nly = presently
pre'ne'r = pretty nearly
pun'ture = puncture
pŭss = purse
put [putt] = two-wheeled cart, **dung put** [or pot]

quar = quarry

rake = reek [for garden rake, reäke]
reck = rack [for holding cattle fodder etc.]
reckon = think
rick = a stack of straw or hay
rout = rut or route
ruf = roof

s is often replaced by *z*. If in doubt, check under both

'satternoon = this afternoon
scrag = the smaller parts of a tree branch [or joint of meat – scrag end]
scram = distorted, twisted, as with cold weather. **Scrammed with cold. Scrammen**
screws = aches and pains
scud = sudden shower of rain
sgin = skin
shard = earthenware, not china
shassen = shall not
shatton = shalt not
shore = prop for securing hurdles at regular intervals
shoulden = should not
sh'ow-crop = shrew mouse
's-know = dost know [**you** is often added : **"Ah, 's-know you"**]
sloo = sloe
smeech = dust
snags = small sloes
sneäke = snake
so = for as [**"I thought so much"**]
spars = forked sticks used in securing thatch, or sparrows. As in **"The spars be a-pullen out the thatch. We could do wi' zome mwore spars t' kip it in"**
spwooän = spoon
s'pwose = suppose
spuddle = dig, as a chicken in search of food
spur = spread – dung over the ground
squäsh = squash
stout = gadfly
sucamore = sycamore

tāe = tea
tahk = talk

terr'ble = terrible "**terr'ble big.**" [the adverb is lost]

tha's = that's, that is

thee = thou and thine: used in rural areas, often ungrammatically; thee, meaning you, often used as your: "**Thee's be gwo'en t' cheänge thee bus at Wimburne**" [**You are are** going to change your bus at Wimborne]. Thy is sometimes used as thee. "**Thee hwome town be Wimburne be it?**" Thou hast is often "**Thee hast.**" Other repetition occurs, ie: "**Thee's can goo be theezelf.**" [You **can can** go by yourself]. There can be strange mixtures: "**Thee cup and thy zaucer.**" Why not use **yours?** the reader may say. Alas, that at times becomes **your'n**

th = Most words in the dialect are with the soft sound, as **the**. As in other dialects *th* often becomes *f*. Breath = **breaf**, filth = **filf**, health = **healf.**

theäse = these

ther' = there

they = them [**all o' they**]

tiddies = potatoes

tidden [or tid'n] = it is not

t'mar = tomorrow

t'other = the other

tissen [or tis'n] = it is not

tooe = toe

trioby = trilby

trōw = trough

't'ould = it would

turmit = turnip

tuth = tooth

'twad'n = it was not [or **'twerd'n,** in broader accent, it were not]

tweil = toil

twite = twit, taunt

'twon't = it won't

t' = to. It should be noted that in speech there is often a mixture and both forms may be used. ie: "**You mid come t' me, or I might come to thee**"

tt = Often in the rural areas with the sound of *dd,* as in **bedder** [better] **madder** [matter] **liddle** [little] **kiddle** [kettle]. Here there are traces of American

ŭvvle = able

v often replaces *f* at the beginning of a word. In the broader dialect the *f* as the first [**virst**] letter is rarely sounded. I have not recorded all the words, but, in general, only those which change after the first letter. Consider 'vile' [loathsome] and file. From its sound phial must also be considered

varden = farthing

vargis = acid. Probably verdigris. "**As sour as vargis**" [varjis]

vark = fork

vaws = vase

veäce = face

veäries = fairies

veller = fellow

ve'ne'r = very nearly
vinny = blue vinny cheese
viren = fuel for fire
vit = feet
vo'k = folk
voller = follow
vurry = very [or furry]
vurzook = forsook
vust = first
vuzz = furze, gorse

v at times becomes *b* and a few words change, seven is an example, seben. Just to make it more difficult, the end also changes, seb'n. Yet more difficult, the *n* becomes *m,* seb'm or seb'mty. Thus in a broad accent one might hear: **"zeb'mty dree".** Other examples are, Heaven, **[Heb'm],** eleven **['leb'm],** oven **[ob'm].** On the whole *v* causes problems. Good advice might be, first make sure it is meant to be *v.*

w often added before *o* as in **wold** [old], **cwold** [cold], **swold** [sold], **fwold** [fold]

wadden = wasn't
war = often pronounced as car
ware = crockery
werden = were not, or was not
whad-'ee-call-it = what do you call it? or, **whad-'ee-m'-call-it [m'** = mid (might)]
wha'f = what have
wha's = what is
wha's'at = what is that. **wha's-'em** = what's them [what are they]
wha's-neäme = what is the name
whe'r = whether
wher' = where
who's-it = who is it
wi' = with
widder = widow
wik = week
will'm = will they
wim or [wimmer] = winnow machine
wĭnder = window
wink = winch, wind, crank
withy = not only the willow branch, but often the tree
woish = wash
wŏnt = mole
woone = one
woun't = won't
woussen = wouldst not, will you not
wops or [wopsy] = wasp
wuss = worse
wust = worst

wutcher = what cheer. Greeting common to other dialects

yaller = yellow
yarn = chat
yé = yes
ye'r = year, or hear
yer = here
yop = yap, yelp
you = often added as in **"mid rain you"** or **"mid rain 'sknow you"** [might rain you know **you**]
you'm = you am, you are
your'n = yours [your one]
yow = ewe

z is often interchangeable with *s* in the broader accent, as in **Darzet** [note the change of *o* to *a*]. Also as above with *c* as, **'zepten** ['cepting, excepting]
zeb'm = seven
zich = such
zim = seem
zīve = scythe
zoo = so
zoss = sauce
zosser = saucer
z'pwose = suppose
zummit = something

Compton Abbas

2

THE VILLAGE nestles in a Dorset valley, and the River Allen runs silently through its centre. Apart from an occasional ripple the flow is as silent as the trout, almost motionless in the shadow of the bridge. Throwing pieces of bread into the shadowy area, soon brought the trout to the surface, but before I used up too many of my sandwiches, meant for dinner, I moved towards the little school. There, imprisoned for the day, I could dream of nature outside and plan for the time between the end of school and dusk, when there were important things with which to be occupied.

My family was, in general, a happy one, but money was not plentiful in the early nineteen thirties, so we made do with many things and did without others. One of the things my mother did without, was as a result of my firm handling of a tricky situation. When I was at my play and out of earshot, my mother used a whistle, much as the teachers at school did, in order to call me from my play. It was quite enough for me to contend with the schoolyard whistle, without having my free time curtailed by a shrill blast long before bedtime. Quite deliberately, and in a calm frame of mind, I took the whistle to the deepest part of the river and, mumbling suitable words, dropped it into the deep. Washing my hands of the whole affair, I continued with my play, mixing mud pies and making patterns on them, then placing them in lines to be baked – frosted and iced – overnight.

Before dark there were the gutters to be blocked again. The gutters were there to drain the water from the bottom of the garden, where I was determined to turn a small pond into a reasonable sea. My mother's voice was eventually heard and for some reason it was more strident than at other times. When I had 'allowed myself' to hear, I came home with my stick, my jar of finds and my inevitable dirty shoes and socks. "The whistle mam?" I answered, when accused. It could only have been me who was guilty of taking it and, to quote my mother, **"Mid [might] as well admit it vust [first] as last."** I did it first and suffered the flat of her hand across my bottom. This was serious enough in the crime category to warrant other penalties, but all that followed was: **"I tell 'ee you must vind'n."** That threat worried me little, as I enjoyed messing about along the river, so I could pretend to look for the whistle. Had my Headmaster known, he would have reported: "Does not try hard enough."

"I han't got zix pairs o' hands," my mother often shouted. She had no need of six pairs, her one pair coped with all our needs, quite often all at the same time. How she watched toast, dressed children, attended to my father and wrote a note to the Headmaster, explaining my absence the day before, I shall never know. I do know that her day was lived at that sort of pace, except for a brief spell at about 3 pm to 4 pm, when she **"put herzelf ztraight,"** and walked through the village with an air of well-being.

Shouting her **"Good addernoons,"** to cottagers, she asked the most intimate questions, yet got polite answers. She was notorious for her blunt remarks: **"They tiddies [potatoes] d' need healen up, or they'll grow out,"** she instructed, or **"Not a bit o' use you whitewashen yur kitchen, 'twill goo brown when the zalt d' come drough."** She was right, the salt did come through and turn the white a dirty brown. The salt had impregnated the bricks over the years, years of hanging sides of bacon from the iron bars, enough to last the family through several months. The curing did little for the decor of the kitchen, but many cottagers were glad of the permanent bacon supply. At the rear of our cottage was a woodshed and a place to keep coal. Behind that shed was a sty for one or two pigs, room for **"vowls"** [poultry] and a garden where lots of vegetables were grown. With milk and fresh butter from the farm, there was a ready supply of food for hungry mouths.

My mother had a habit of shouting the things that should have been whispered, that is, should they have been said at all. **"'Tis gwoen t' be a bwoy, you'm round like a barrel."** A laugh from the mother-to-be and a grimace from us children, who could only look on quietly. My mother's most embarrassing performance was in the Market Place at Ringwood. **"Come on,"** she would say, **"Le's git on inta Ring'ood,"** and off we went down the road to wait for the bus.

The ten mile journey was painful too. My mother chatted to those she knew, but worse, to those she did not. She prefaced her remarks: **"You must be wold Jack So and So's daughter?"** An almost involuntary nod proved my mother right, so she gleamed and continued: **"I thought as much, what used t' live t'other zide o' Wimburne?"** My mother was away and nothing would stop her. She drained or wrenched all the information she required and repeated it very loudly for the benefit of the other passengers. Pretending to be asleep was my escape, for I knew at some point we should have, **"An' this is my bwoy."** It was a relief to arrive at Ringwood, but that was short-lived. Having viewed the toy shops and the mouth-watering cake shops, "Oh mam, let's have some of them," **"No, there's nothen in 'em,"** she always replied in her practical way. "There is mam, there is, there's jam and there's ....." My reply was lost as I was dragged into the Market Place, where humiliation waited.

Oddments of material, that was my mother's craze. **"Jist do vur the kitchen winder** [window]," she said, spotting a piece of material suitable for curtains. The humiliation began when her method of trading commenced. Deciding on the material she required, she picked it up from the front of the stall and moved to the boxes of smaller oddments at the rear. Holding her piece firmly underneath the large pile in the box, so that no scrabbling hand would claw her precious find, she began her selling. Pulling out piece by piece of material, she held them up for the crowd of shoppers to admire. **"Nice piece this, dirt cheap, zixpence,"** or **"This piece vur wonly a zhillen."** So time wore on, till my mother was satisfied that all around were aware of her. Indeed, who could not have been? Pulling out her piece and holding it up with great scorn, she asked: **"How much do 'ee want vur this?"** "Two zhillen," the stallholder replied. Then followed my mother's performance.

With all the effort employed by Mrs Siddons, she began, **"Two zhillen, you must be joken. Two zhillen vur that bit o' rubbish, two zhillen vrom a poor zoul who have bin an' zwold half yur goods fur y'?"** I knew the pattern so well, as she engaged the sympathy of other shoppers: **"Didden I vind you a bargain, didden I zell you that, zurely I've earned a little bit off?"** She was clever enough not to allow the stallholder to interject: **"Goo on then, have it vor a zhillen"** – oh no, my mother may have embarrassed us, but her timing was perfect. Near to tears and breaking point, holding the material to her, she lowered her voice almost to a sob, **"Vancy chargen zomebody who has ......"** By this time the crowd of shoppers did as required: **"Give it to her, y' mean wold so** an' so," they choroused, and as he did so, the close observer might have seen the gleam in my mother's eyes, as she "went into the wings." We cringed and crept away, furious at her display, but deep down admiring her skill.

The bus journey home could be humiliating too, depending on circumstances. Our shopping was carefully covered up, so that no one could **gap** [look] at it, but if other passengers showed just a little of their purchases, it was an opening for my mother: **"Didden have any o' they, too dear I thought,"** or **"There were zome better woones than they in the Co-op."** Direct insult was not beyond her: **"I didden have none o' they tomater plants, 'cos they looked too zpindly. Then you dwon't do much gard'nen, do 'ee?"** She sometimes softened the blow, if that is how one can see it, with: **"I can let 'ee have zome better plants."**

Arriving home, there would be a certain amount of gloating to endure, as she inspected her bargains. Then a cup of tea with rather special cakes, but not those of my choosing. My new shoes had to be fitted again – **"Jist t' be zure."** Feeling rather proud, I asked if I might keep them on and go out to play. **"Noo you can't, they'm vur Zundays,"** was her firm instruction.

Sunday clothes were Sunday clothes, and were to be worn only on Sundays and even then, just for going places in. If one stayed home, or on the return home, off came the Sunday clothes. When did Sunday clothes become weekday clothes? On Whit Sunday. This was the time for a completely new outfit, a time when ladies especially, with the summer ahead, thought of new and nicer things to wear. The church played some part in this, as many an outfit was first worn to church on Whit Sunday. Proof of this is that many of the women's dresses and costumes were in white, the colour associated with the church at Whitsuntime. Girls' dresses were less restricted in colour and were often chosen from a mail-order catalogue. The little girls portrayed in the catalogues appeared to be dolls, rather than girls. Real girls in the advertised dresses never looked quite the same. All the mail-order firms seemed to be in Liverpool or Manchester, a fact that I understood more clearly when my schooling took in the textile industry.

In summer the family seemed to spread out more and were together so very little. My father in the fields in daylight hours, my mother helping on the farm or in the garden and my sister Iris playing on the pathway outside the front door. When winter came all were in one room, the room in which a large fire burned. By its warmth we toasted cheese, and with many "oohs" and "ahs" we pulled out hot jacketed potatoes from its ashes. My sister and I were often put to bed a little earlier just before Christmas, as **"there be things to attend to."** One night we were allowed to wait up with mam as my father went to get something for Christmas dinner. He walked about four miles to a farm in the next village, where it was possible to buy cheaply a turkey, or if funds were low, a couple of chickens. As dad set out on that cold windy night, I gathered from the conversation it was to be chicken that year. There were at least two calls on the way, one or two healths to be drunk at the farm, with other friends and greetings to be attended to on the way home.

Nine o'clock was late and my mother had wound the clock, pushing the hands forward another five minutes. **"'Tis better t' be too early, than t'other way about,"** she commented. So, the Victorian mantel clock stayed fifteen minutes fast, but as everybody *knew* it to be fast, I could not see the advantage. At last my father arrived, swaying a little, "Perhaps because of the fierce wind," I thought. In his pocket was a bottle of stout, which my mother put into the larder, as if it were sinful that it be seen by children. I delayed my cheese and baked potato as long as possible, pretending to drink my cocoa, so that dad's account of the evening could be heard. **"Met wold Harry,"** he said, with a happy smile, **"He wansh t' know if you're shtill ash perty ash when he lash shaw y',"** he spluttered. **"Nonsense,"** said my mother, severely. **"Ish not nonshense,"** he said, **"Ish true,"** as my mother took a large sacking bag from him.

"Got 'ee woone," said my father, with some pride. **"Only one?"** my mother accused. He agreed there was only one. **"We always have two, one's not enough."** **"Harry said woone ish plenty,"** he replied, **"Everybody jish hash woone."** **"I don't care what others have,"** fumed my mother, heading for what my father used to call a **"humdinger of a row."** **"One is no use to us, one chicken for a family's not enough,"** she added hotly. [It is interesting to note that when mother was cross, she 'came out' of her accent, presumably to be less 'familiar.'] My father steadied himself to deliver: **"Woone goosh ish."** My mother's voice had ascended in pitch: **"I tell you one is not ..."** – Her argument stopped mid stream, as she went to check the contents of the sack, coming back with a broad grin, which produced a satisfied, though vacant smile on my father's face. This was the time for little children to go to the upper – and colder – regions of the house. **"I zhall be up in two or dree minutes to zee if you'm in bed,"** said my mother calmly. We were soon asleep, happy in the knowledge that peace reigned in the kitchen and that on Christmas Day we were to have goose. Few of the cottagers had goose, so this Christmas was going to be rather special.

Walking a long distance to find holly with lots of berries was not a rewarding pastime, when on arrival it was found that the gipsies had cut away most of the tree and the holly was probably on sale in Blandford Market. However, we knew spots deep in the wood, where holly was to be found. I cannot remember failing to find holly with berries, nor can I remember any picture in the sitting-room without at least two pieces of holly lodged over its frame.

Had my parents kept straight faces when telling me of Father Christmas, I might have believed, instead of half believing. My imagination tried to grasp the fact that one man in a red cloak and whiskers, visited every house. My world was small, but it seemed impossible that one man, no matter how kind and generous with his time, could descend so many chimneys in one evening; it might have taken him the whole of Christmas Eve to find the right chimney at the Manor. I thought it rather sad that he never called on gran. With a twinkle, she said: **"He do wonly call on good childern."**

Wood was chopped, so there would be plenty for the cold days ahead. **"Never put the hook [chopper] on table, 'tis terr'ble bad luck,"** my mother pleaded, **"Bezides, the childern mid [might] cut their vingers on'n,"** she added. **"They'd never cut theirzelves on 'ee [it],"** my father boasted, **"You could ride t' Lon'on an' back on 'ee."** Besides superstitions, there were other things to observe, such as weather predictions: **"Fog on the hill brings water to the mill,"** and **"Fog on the moor brings sunshine to the door."** Fairly common was: **"Rain before seven, clear up before eleven,"** and in the evening: **"'Twill clear up for the whores."** What were whores? Later in my education I learned that they were not very creditable women and the operative time was 9 pm.

3

BILL BAILEY **won't you please come hwome."** My mother looked sadly at the garden gate, which also led to the cottage next door, then at us. **"They woon't zing that round yer for a long time t' come,"** she said. At the age of five it was not easy to understand the horror of death, or indeed the finality of it, but I knew that 'dying' meant not being seen again. Mr Bailey was the man next door, who was often called Bill, and was a familiar figure climbing into his little van, having piled the children into the back and driving off, as he had done earlier that day. It was the day before Christmas Eve and he with his family had gone shopping in the nearby town of Blandford.

There was the strangeness of the silence next door and the occasional utterence from my mother, **"Oh dear God, no."** It was some time before the facts filtered through to me. I gathered that the van had got out of control on the return journey and half way down a hill, overturned and caught fire. The rest of the story I grasped in the hurried whispers as various people called. **"Poor little mites, trapped in the back ...."** and **"Oranges rolled down the hill ...."** Oranges made me aware of Christmas again, for there would be one in my stocking. One, because there was little money from my father's wage of thirty shillings a week, to buy a great deal of any item regarded as a luxury.

It is only in growing older that death is understood as an important part of childhood and the preparation for maturity. The death of grandparents is normally the child's first experience of loss and perhaps the first realisation that things happen to us and not only to others. *My friends may die, but not I.* There is a saying in Dorset: **"A blaren cow do zoon vorget her calf."** Children's minds are soon bent on other things, as were ours on Christmas and who should have this or that from the good things hung on the mistletoe. There were pink and white candy mice, chocolate shapes of pure fascination and things wrapped in shiny paper. **"Can I have the clock mam, can I, can I, can I have the clock mam?"** **"We'll zee,"** came the sensible reply. Soon after Christmas the mistletoe was stripped and in perfect fairness, all honour satisfied.

In later years when it was more normal to have a Christmas tree, I realised that mistletoe was free and could be 'taken' from its resting place. Stealing a Christmas tree from the thousands in the woods surrounding the village, would have meant being **"chucked out o' house an' hwome,"** Snaring a pheasant, though it strutted behind you, taking out the broad beans as they were planted, would have had the same effect.

The Dorset dialect has always been very dear to me, but as a child I was often misled by the sound of words. I was, on occasions, allowed to wander across the field to another cottage, where a dear lady whom I loved, let me climb on a chair, in order to reach her tall dresser, on which were many rows of pickled delights. She and I both knew my favourite was pickled red cabbage. The taste today brings her to mind and I see her 'farmhouse' expression, half way between a smile and pure satisfaction as I ate greedily. Mrs Martin was a sweet soul, if ever one existed. Except that her name was not Martin, but Norton. The *o* becomes *a* in the dialect and the *N* was simply misheard. To me she is still Mrs Martin, for if that name is destroyed, then so is one of my most pleasant memories.

Winter in the village brought much mud to the roads, which were of flint, laid and simply rolled in by steam-roller. Much dust was produced during dry periods and when the rains came, it lay in puddles across the roads. When tar macadam came the roads appeared to be much wider and were more comfortable, both for vehicles and pedestrians. During very hard winters the River Allen froze quite solid and it was possible to slide most of the way to school.

Horror plays an important part in the young mind. It was common for many children, brought up in the shadow of the Victorian era, to know fear. Fear, both in religious and family matters, was an important, though mistaken ingredient in a child's upbringing. Both my mother and my grandmother warned me before, during and after most of my crimes, **"You'll zee the wold Nick"** [The Devil]. Not impressed, or in any way horrified by a visit from Satan, in fact I felt a meeting might be interesting, I merely scoffed at their description of the Devil: **"A little wold man, not as tall as you,"** they said, **"An ugly gnarled dwarf, with"** and they emphasized, **"eyes like saucers."** This was repeated, with more sinister implications each time. "Nonsense," I thought, till the day arrived, when in the view of my betters, a felony of mammoth proportions was committed. I had removed the lid from an old tin trunk and put to sea in it. When I say, put to sea, I should explain that my ocean was a few inches deep and rather muddy at that, and in case the reader is thinking of Lyme Regis or Weymouth, my sea was at the bottom of the garden.

I launched my ship, but on climbing in, realized how bad a sailor I was when it capsized, before making any part of the voyage possible. You may imagine the state of my school clothes and the wrath of my mother. I was put to bed after a sound thrashing and thorough cleaning. Tearful, I lay looking towards the door of the bedroom. The knob, and there is no doubt in my mind, slowly turned and, with an equal lack of doubt in my seeing, there stood the Devil. Exactly as described, he stood, his saucer eyes gazing directly at me. Whether I fainted I cannot say, but I was a more subdued little boy for some time after. Not completely subdued, for a child with imagination can rarely be quelled by fear.

The child psychologist might suggest that humour be introduced in the explanation of the forces of nature, but alas, that does not always work. My grandmother presented humorous word pictures to explain, as she put it **"God's work,"** Thunder was easy: **"All that nise** [noise]," she said wisely, as she sucked her almost toothless gums, **"Be the angels up there, moven that zofa about."** Thinking of it today, it is a fairly apt description of the sound. At that impressionable age, the story was fixed in my mind, to be brought out on the day of a violent storm. As the thunder commenced, I looked towards the barbed wire fence at the end of the field. It was possible to open the wire and so let vehicles through. In the semi-darkness of the storm, the wire opened and a black leather covered sofa trundled into view. Petrified by my vision, I was transfixed, till being told not to be silly. In Dorset as in other places it is possible to hear a 'tall' story told with a straight face. Perhaps children should be spared this sort of joke, or even have it told them as a fairy story.

I was not fond of school and in the afternoon prayed for thunder. I knew if thunder was about, my mother would say: **"We'm gwoen t' have zome weather,"** and come to fetch me in good time. My infant school-teacher was willing to release me in exchange for a little local gossip. She was a Victorian in every way, but an excellent teacher, and I have much to be grateful for in learning the hard lessons she taught. She recoiled in horror at the sound from a **"dirty mouth,"** whether lies or foul language, and her penalty for this offence, which I so often committed, was a good washing out of the mouth with carbolic. In my wrong doing today, I am reminded of the taste and take care. In the middle of a lesson she stopped abruptly, and with her nose in the air, her eyes accusing him who looked guilty, she delivered: **"Some person has broken wind."** With great deliberation, she took a large spill of newspaper, lit it and held it aloft. Gazing intently at him who must be guilty, who, with enough power, she might have burnt at the stake, as she intoned: **"That should get rid of the excess gases and the horrid odour."** My great failing has always been a guilty look, except when at my most guilty.

If emotion ever wells up in the adult as in the child, then the sight or taste of cream crackers will awaken great emotion within me. She was a good teacher, gentle, but insistent on discipline; even infants had to be aware of their place. The cream crackers had been found in the class-room and, holding them up, she cried: **"Who has lost these?"** There was a long pause and no child put in a claim. I knew the taste of cream crackers, an absolute luxury, so I felt I must have them, especially as no other child seemed sensible or hungry enough to stake a claim. **"They're mine, Miss,"** I said, and immediately regretted it. She paused, holding the little packet aloft, her eyes told me, as mine her, the real truth. She smiled and, handing me the biscuits said: **"There you are Jimmy, now eat them up, while we wait for you."** At that moment, I wanted to laugh, cry, eat carefully, gobble, or simply sink into the floor, instead I munched, gulping back tears, while my stern teacher and the class looked on with somewhat manufactured sympathy. If humiliation is good for a child, then at that moment I was indeed a paragon.

Not all my infant school moments were as painful. There were things to treasure for a lifetime. My first hearing and learning of poetry was such a moment. "Jimmy is a born actor," said the Headmaster and in later years I went on to fulfill his prophesy. Poetry at that young age needed to be dramatic and I knew it was important to stress particular words. The poem in question described the losing and finding of a doll, while playing on the heath. "I *lost* my poor little doll dears .... " I knew without question the important word in the verse and the sadness to be conveyed in that word. The more emphasis laid there, then the more effective the next verse: "I *found* my poor little doll dears .... " Perhaps the important thing surrounding that poem was the fact that I did not, nor had I any desire to own a doll, and had I been forced to take one on the heath to play, I would most certainly have *lost* it dears. Paramount, is the actor taking his role. This was a girl's poem, but I knew that and adapted to the part, still getting the maximum out of the little drama. "Jimmy is a born actor," and I have that in writing. A born actor, but alas, no scholar.

The piano in the infants' class-room should really have been ashamed of the title. Imagine the worst possible honky-tonk instrument, and the sound of the middle of the keyboard, that would be the upper register of the infants' piano. I knew there was much wrong with it, but assumed that the blind man who came to tune it, was in some way at fault in not seeing which strings to tighten. All of them seemed very loose indeed. Yet the piano in the music room was perfectly pitched, so the tuner man must have known quite a lot about pianos. I remember word for word and note by note, my first song learned from my Victorian teacher; it was of course a Victorian song:

"Oh the merry month of leafy June,
When the world is fresh and fair,
And the birds all sing their songs in tune,
When the music fills the air" ... and so on.

The sound of that piano, those terrible verses, the taste of carbolic and the smell of, or rather the sight of a burning newspaper spill, created a hard beginning to learning, but I am grateful for the tough moments.

Released from school, which to me was some sort of prison, I scuffed my way through the dust to our cottage, where my mother might well have greeted me: **"You do need zome new zhoes, where the money's comen vrom I dwon't know."** I had my new shoes and I will tell you where the money came from.

"Tis vive o'clock and time you were all up," my mother yelled. This meant we were off to the fields to do some of the hardest work I have seen women engaged in. **"I want t' take in the vield avore wold Mother so an' so,"** my mother shouted defiantly. We trudged a mile to the field, then started to pick up the scattered flints, after the sheep had eaten down the root crop. Taking the area with the best stones, we picked up the larger ones and carried the very heavy buckets to make piles, which we measured with a yard string. With a point at the apex of the pile, a measured yard was more quickly produced, but at 9 am when the contractor arrived with his lorry, he flattened all our points, which meant yet more buckets of stones. One yard of stones reduced the hands to roughened shapes, and in time they were more like claws. A Dorset expression, **"clawen up stwones,"** confirms that. For the morning's work we received a few shillings. That is where the money came from for my new shoes, **"wi' me ztwone-picken zhillens."** Next morning the rival woman would be up before light, ready to do battle in **"clawen up the stwones."**

My first watch came from **"docken."** Before the corn grew too high, docks had to be weeded out, which meant tiny hands and arms pulling very hard, till the hands were black and blue. This was slave-labour, as the farmer paid one penny a hundred, but children did not, nor do they think in those terms if something desirable can be achieved. That watch, so hard-earned, was treasured. **"Wonly Marks and Zpencers,"** they gibed, but it was a precious five bob object to me.

They were **"wold-fashioned"** days and the cottages with their well kept gardens were a matter of pride to the villagers. I, with many others, must break our hearts at the sight of these cottages and gardens now. **"I zhould like a bit o' that,"** was so often heard from the next garden. The sharing continued, till at no cost, each cottager boasted very beautiful flowers. My mother was, she said, **"Very vond o' tenwick stocks."** I was quite a big boy before I had sorted out the dialect from that statement. **"Tenwick"** is of course "ten-week" – then all becomes clear. March blew its way into April, **"One month do goo half into t'other,"** they said, and after some study I am inclined to agree. So April showers continued into May. **"Ne'r cast a clout till May is out,"** they chimed, sometimes in unison. Then came the tease, **"Mind 'ee, noobody do zay whether it be May the month, or may the vlower"** [hawthorn blossom].

They did not debate the matter, showing the dryness of the Dorset humour, in that, if nothing is black and white, it could be spoken of with a twinkle, then left well alone.

The village hall was still a place for entertainment, the 'social' being the high spot of the week. My first experience of sadism must have been when they insisted that a young man, with the broadest accent, should perform, **"The vlies be on the turmit tops."** They laughed at him because of his *normal* dialect. I felt sorry for him, as he, oblivious, monologued through his piece. Even simple country folk can be cruel.

The village had its own band and very good it was too. With a full range of instruments it led processions around the village when so required for carnivals and other events. On Saturdays the same band played for a dance which was held in the village hall. Such was the power of the church, that just before midnight and certainly not after, the last waltz had been waltzed and the last goodnights shouted abroad, or cooed into shell-like ears, as the peace of Sunday descended upon the cluster of little houses, while each candle was extinguished. Tired labouring limbs stretched for a few hours till the church bells called them to confess their Saturday sin. Could sin be committed in such a close community? It would seem so, forgiveness should be sought for failing to raise the hat to the Lady of the Manor who was revered, and that is not too strong a word. There was a private walk from the manor to the church, *Ladies Walk*. No living person who was not a lady could walk that way, nor ever did. The reader should not confuse 'lady' with 'woman', there is a great difference. This lady commanded – and I choose the word carefully – respect. There were people within the congregation, who when in church, admired *Her* chapel – the Lady Chapel. This, with a fine statue of the Madonna at its entrance.

She it was who loved animals, some said more than people, and she it was who would go to the ends of the earth to root out an offender who dealt the smallest amount of cruelty to any animal. **"Zhe got the posh** [money]," the locals said. They were right, she could have produced a cool million and property in Dorset, London and Ireland besides. "Send him to me," she ordered. A gardener who was living in sin with his housekeeper, stood in front of her desk the next morning. "Get married at once," she bellowed. They did, in as much time as was necessary for banns to be called. Had he failed to carry out her instructions, he would have been told to leave his cottage and his work. This meant a removal beyond the county, to some spot where a reference was not essential.

The power of the manor and the power of the church were bound closely. The Lord of the manor suggested to the Bishop, who got the right priest for the church, a priest of high tradition, who raised the quality of ceremonial beyond the level the surrounding villages could hope to attain. I have seen and worshipped in churches in most parts of the world, and in many of them missed the beauty and sanctity of my village church. At its altar I served the priest, that holy man who lies in a grave under a yew tree, just beyond the East window. If I need to find myself, find peace, that which passeth man's understanding, that is where my feet will take me.

4

JUST BEFORE leaving the infants' class, I created one last little drama so that I would be remembered. Within the class, one boy who was a cripple, found it difficult to rest in the sitting position for a long spell, so had an air-filled cushion on which he reclined. It was always a source of interest and for me especially so. I needed to inspect it, which led my devilish thoughts to tampering, and in the end I let the air out of it. He complained bitterly, till my teacher asked that the culprit be found. "Jimmy, Miss," they all cried. Normally a special pump was used to inflate the cushion, but on this occasion, amid floods of tears, I had to blow the thing up with my own breath. Sobbing, complaining that all present had enjoyed the joke, I was forced to reinflate the cushion. My first lesson in knowing, "Those with you, are not necessarily behind you."

Even my last day as an infant was overshadowed by a sort of class distinction. We had all been asked to read, recite, or sing something during that last afternoon, and I decided on singing something I knew well, having been taught it at my mother's knee. She, in her younger years, was a member of the Salvation Army. No one in the village could dream of belonging to anything other than the Church of England. My mother had become C of E, and my song, was after all, just a little song. My teacher's eyes told me after the first line, that I had committed something akin to sacrilege in my rendering of the foot-tapping, tamberine-bashing song. *"Whosoever will, whosoever will,"* I began, as the rest of the class leaned forward. Not only was Jimmy singing an odd song, but it was in a foreign language! *"Spread the blesséd tidings all the world around, whosoever will, shall come,"* Stony silence; with me just standing there. A silence broken by my teacher's command: "Thank you Jimmy, that was – was – very nice." I crept back to my seat, rather glad I had not decided to sing a lullaby I had been taught, which in my memory went as follows: *Go to sleep my little piccaninny, I shall have to whick you whack you if you don't, go to sleep, close your eyes, mother's little baby, daddy's little* [wait for it] *ally-qually-quoo.* Heaven knows what they would have made of that! "Anyway," I thought, "even that was better than rotten old *Golden Slumbers.*"

New coat pegs next term a different toilet and wash-basins, different everything. I visualised it all with some horror and trepidation, but next term was a long way from that Friday and there was lots to cram in between. Three thirty and prayers: "Our Father **WHICH** art **IN** Heaven, Hallowed **BE** Thy name ...." "Odd," I thought, even then; "how we, unless we *feel* the words, emphasize the wrong ones."

The journey home from school should have taken half an hour, but two hours was my average for the completion of the most interesting part of my school day. In the paddock, which I must cross on my way home, were the ponies, waiting to be fed. In my satchel were several sandwiches which should have been eaten at dinner-time, but somehow, jam sandwiches, so often gooseberry, were not very appetising when they had been hanging around for a time. The jam seemed to seep through and make the bread rather soggy. Jam, especially blackcurrent, should *sit* on top of the bread and allow the teeth to meet it before the actual eating begins. **"You can't have bwoff** [both]," my parents said. We came to accept that bread would have butter or jam, rarely both. This takes me to the subject of cake. There was not always cake, but there would be on Sunday without fail.

"You must ate yer brade an' butter vust [first]," they said. We munched through as quickly as possible, eyeing our piece of cake. There would be a pause before attacking it, perhaps to remember the adage: **"You can't have your cake and eat it."**

Feeding the ponies my sandwiches was an enjoyable pastime, and just a little of the delaying action I employed before my mother began the search for me, but that was hours away. Over the stile and I followed the footpath across **'leb'm** [eleven] acres, with occasional deviations for some daisies, **gilcups** [buttercups], or even a butterfly. The footpath was well used as a short-cut from one part of the village to the other. I must return to death for a moment, to show how important a part it played in village life. I do not know if there is any legal foundation in what follows, but there is no doubt it was law for the villagers and for the local farmers. It was always said, in rather severe and reverent tones, that if a corpse had been carried over a particular area that was not already a right of way, then the path followed became a public footpath. 'leb'm acres had such a path and was used by all who travelled on foot. The farmer planted the field, leaving the path, so that he ended up with two triangles of crop to be harvested.

The path ended in the corner of the field near the chalk pit. Chalk had been taken from the area some years before, leaving a large hollow. **'Dwon't goo up chalk pit,"** I was warned, which of course was an invitation to do so. The danger lay in the edges of the pit, which might have given way, but more important, the pit was used as a rubbish dump. To me, rubbish was, and still is, fascinating. Much time was spent in the search for things, with the danger of poisons or broken glass pushed firmly into the background. My find[s] were clutched close and carried home, only to end up in another rubbish tip, after my hands, dirty as they were, had received a couple of smart slaps.

Next on my list to visit were the cress-beds. On a hot summer's day, lying prone, with my face dipped towards the spring which supplied the beds, was a cooling experience, and still is, even in memory. Cupping the hands and supping the clear cool water was an invigorating break in my after-school tour. The sight of a kingfisher near the cress-beds was an added bonus.

One must always have a parasol for the sun, or an umbrella for the rain. Just at the bend of the road by the river bank were tall and wide-leaved wild rhubarb. Excellent for shielding the hot sun from tired little heads, or to keep off the occasional shower. Time did not exist, so why not a deviation over the swampland to where the swans were to be found? It had been drummed into me that I must avoid them at nesting time. It was possible, they said, to be killed by the force of an attacking swan. Studying them at close quarters, I could well believe the warning.

Returning to the road, in case mam came to meet me, was my next thought. No need to hurry, everything must be checked and noted for a further inspection. The wind was behind me, as on my hands and knees, in the middle of the road, I began my inspection of the skeleton of a leaf. The once complete leaf was fascinating in detail. I felt something touch my knees, something that was not the roadway, not my satchel, or my collection of flowers and empty tins. It was moving very slowly, made of metal and pushing my knees, pushing very slightly. It was difficult to ignore the rusted chrome bar, and, about to touch it, I looked up to see the fishmonger's van behind it. It was the van's bumper! Seeing a sinister grin on the face of the man who brought the bloaters for tea, I collected myself and ran. I could not understand what he was laughing about, after all, this might have been a fatal accident!

I paused for a while in my flight, to make sure the geese from the farm were not just at the farmyard gate. All was quiet and because I was a little frightened of the gander, I did a quick sprint past the gateway. Out they came, screaming as if they had never seen me before, but I was a safe distance and reduced my speed to a stroll again. Through the fence, sustaining no rents, and into the orchard, and, looking innocent, grabbed a few apples. I bore right along the hedge of the garden behind the little thatched cottage. It was a pretty and well kept garden which I had studied many times before. Thou shalt not covet, I had been taught, thy neighbour's ox, nor his ass, oh and lots of other things. Thou shalt not covet thy neighbour's alarm clock. I had never heard that before. There was no ox in the garden, no ass, but there was an alarm clock. Hanging on a nail outside the woodshed the alarm clock had been for many weeks, abandoned, but not quite thrown away. I paused to admire it again, then moved quickly down the hill on the last few yards before home. I knew I should return at some time to admire the alarm clock, and that it would be the focal point of some event in my future.

Pausing near the last cottage but one, to get a glimpse of the boy who was "not quite all there," so they said, I saw him wobbling his head back and forth and yelling, "Jimmy." Still walking, but now at a brisker pace, I wobbled my head back. At the last thatched cottage before ours, I tried to see the old lady who lived there with her large family. I had seen her once only, dressed all in black. No sign of her. Thought, "How can I be sure she is still there, if she does not appear?"

I could see my mother scanning the distance for sight of me and having spotted my approach, pretending to do some weeding. As usual I crept up on her and cried, "Boo," and as usual, she jumped, saying, **"I wish you woulden do that."** She seemed to have stopped weeding and was going inside to continue preparing tea, all the time calling at me, **"Where have you been all this time?"** She, pretending to be cross, me pretending to be contrite, till my father arrived, then I could escape to my own world. It would be his turn for, **"You're late, what kept you?"**

My father spoke in fairly broad dialect and because of that some of his explanations were rather odd. On this occasion he made his excuse plain with the use of one word: **"Cooler."** That was the milk cooler. It looked rather like a washboard with rubber hose pipes at each end. Cold water ran through it as a radiator, and the milk trickled down the grill as a waterfall, cooling before it reached the churn. If this went wrong, milking of the cows was delayed and, as a result, all other work that followed. **"Cooler"** – everyone knew about. However if he were delayed in the village, it was probably due to meeting someone and stopping for **"a yarn"** [chat]. The classic of my father's replies was: **"I passed Passon** [parson], **an' didden know 'twere Passon till I'd pass'n"** [passed him].

We moved from the cottage at the top of the field to the little bungalow near the road and within a few feet of the river. On a Saturday afternoon my father **"barried"** [borrowed] a horse and cart and moved the furniture to our new home, while my mother moved the smaller items. Pushing a large pram with my sister Iris in it, plus china, bed linen, wall brackets and so on, we moved carefully across the field to the roadway. Sitting in the pram on one of the journeys was a pair of Edwardian vases. Brown and blue with a touch of gold, they were and are, ugly, but precious. Precious because they were part of the pattern of my childhood, and so much happiness or anguish was played out below the mantel shelf which held them.

So near the river, the bungalow was damp at most times of the year. Its rear wall was solid chalk, as were so many houses in Dorset, often a mixture of chalk, flint and bricks. At the end of a passageway, off which were other bedrooms, was a large room, which should have been a sitting-room, but became my bedroom. It had a small fire-place, on each side of which was a large cupboard, which were used for storing apples and potatoes.

The smell of stored apples is one thing, the storage of several hundredweights of **tiddies** [potatoes] is another. Stored in those cupboards and only fifty yards from the farm's grain barn, was a temptation the many farm rats could not resist. In the night they came, having gnawed through the chalk wall. I lay awake listening to the gnawing, not knowing at what point they would get through to the potatoes. The village at this time had no electricity, so the only way to overcome the terror I knew, lying there in the darkness, was to make a noise. Sometimes, though tired from the day's work, my parents rose to assure me: **"They woon't git in,"** but I would not be assured. Nothing would convince me that rats, if not frightened away, would not eat their way through. Oddly I never saw a rat inside the house. Fear, especially in a child, depends on the circumstances. In the grain barn I spent hours playing and watching the rats play. Rats at play are fascinating, close by in a darkened room they are nothing short of a nightmare.

It is possible that the home-made wine, also stored in the cupboards, scared the rats away. Potent, is a mild word for some of the wines my father produced. I remember them with pleasure, especially as they seemed to have a calming effect on him. Some would have said his face carried a rather simple smile, but I prefer to think of him being transported from his mundane workaday life to the heaven of the imagination. My mother sometimes went with him – but alas her smile was often overshadowed by a guilty look, refusing my father's offer of, **"Jist a tiddly drop mwore."** I thanked God for home-made wines, because during the night, corks popped off like rapid machine-gun fire and bottles exploded as Molotov cocktails. That must have kept some rats away.

When all the potatoes had been eaten – was there ever a dinner without? – and all the wine had been drunk, there should have been peace in my bedroom. Not so, for in between the two cupboards there was a small fire-place. Rarely lit, except at times of illness, its chimney had a metal plate inside to stop draughts. To that cosy cavity came the jackdaws. Noisily they came and with much rejoicing. I believe in 'live and let live,' but squawking jackdaws at six in the morning are not to be recommended. Shouting down the echo chamber, "We are moving in, we are moving in," as they dropped sticks down the chimney to build their nest a few feet from my reclining head – when not raised to listen for the crying of baby jackdaws – brought from me the plea to light a fire in the grate. **"Can't waste viren** [fuel] **on a vew wold jackdaws,"** my mother said. My only recourse was to stand in the garden and shout insults at them. They merely dropped more twigs down the chimney and squawked worse things back at me.

Pots of home-made jam were nicer than **"zhop-bought."** Plums from our plum orchard (unusual for Dorset, and as part of a cottage garden) were turned into jam, as were the gooseberries and the blackcurrants. How we children hated the topping and tailing, but how we enjoyed the jam during the winter months. If we ran out of jam before the next fruit season and were forced to buy, my mother avoided a particular brand, made locally. It was checked and verified that the company used swedes and turnips as a base, and actually employed staff in making small wood chippings to represent raspberry pips. Cheap the jam was, but that was the only compliment it could be paid. In these days of trading standards, this could not occur.

Summers remembered from childhood are generally hot, sunny and very long. Freedom is the thing I remember most. Doors and windows wide open, a fire set up in the garden, alfresco style, because it was too hot for he kitchen range. The rare pure yellow cream, made into ice-cream, and even clear fresh water from the well. Summer then, was indicated by women in summer dresses. Nowadays dress is less distinctive. A woman, especially a country woman, brought summer with her in her dress, and I wondered why men had not the same effect. Apart from the cricket field, and cricketers are entirely separate animals, men do not bring the gaiety of summer into anybody's life. Summer, and walks along the dried-up river bed, summer, with sweet peas and asparagus fern, summer, with new bread and blackcurrant jam, and summer, because it was a holiday that stretched ahead almost forever.

Our grandmother came in the summer. From the next village she came, down the narrow stone-littered road, which, during the winter was the river bed, carrying the water from the source of the Allen. Picking her way over the flints, she came towards us, holding out her hands as we met. Carefully she trod the flint road, to avoid hurting her corn-ridden feet, her canvas shoes cut away to allow the corns to protrude, and chatting away as if she were a child herself. The lisping noises she made because of the lack of teeth, made her the more endearing. Gran was sweet. Dressed in black, including a large hat with cherries on it, a walking stick with a springbok horn as a handle, and always ready to listen to our endless chatter. To each she gave four farthings, with which we bought a fair number of sweets. I loved gran, and the little house where she lived. There, she passed her time, surrounded by fine old furniture and china. From a cage in the next garden, a magpie spoke to passers-by, but best of all, there were chocolate slot-machines across the road. We lied to the shopkeeper, saying we had put our pennies in and nothing came out. She smiled and gave us a penny bar (very thin) of chocolate. We ran to tell gran and she smiled too.

Sturminster Newton

5

WHEN SUMMER ended, I mean by that the first week of September, freedom also ended. There was a shadow over the blue of the sky and the gold of the sun. That shadow was the winter of the unknown, the new class-room, the new children, the new desk and all the things that went with it, but, worst of all, a new teacher. A sterner Victorian, but still an excellent teacher. Rest her in Heaven, for she must be there, with her husband who played the church organ, played? **"'ee do meake'n talk,"** they said. Rest her, wherever she is, for she taught me how to enjoy words. Drilled into me that words were not questions and answers, but a mixture of all shades between those two categories.

"Mam says sometimes that it's a delicious day," I piped up. "Does she indeed?" said my teacher, "Then your mam – mother is very wrong. Listen all of you, the word delicious is never used, except in reference to food or drink, is that quite understood?" "Yes Miss." "Yes Miss – Yes Miss – Yes Miss; No Miss," I mumbled. My mother said and did things differently and though I knew there must be a right and wrong way, so often the wrong way was much more attractive. Rest her though, for her stringent guidelines. Rules must be adhered to, but the exceptions should be explored.

Reciting poetry was now an art form. None of your, "Jack and Jill went up the hill," with the monotonous incantations on the pattern of "tum-ti-tum-ti-tum-ti-tum." So, I began, "Old Meg she was a gipsy, she lived upon the mwores," "No, no, no, no," cried my teacher, "Where did Meg live?" "On the mwores, Miss," I repeated. "She did not live on the mwores, she lived on the moors, say it as you would dour, moor, moor, moor. Other similar words are, poor and door. Large 'O's, moor, moor, moor." I considered all she had said, or rather enunciated, and agreed it was sound – and I knew about puns – sound advice. Nothing to it, I thought, but she had only just begun. We were slowly to be taken to bits, word by word and line by line, then reassembled. "Why," I mused, "teach little children, as the new infants were now being taught next door?" I shuddered to think of all the un-teaching that lot would need. *"I lost my poor little doll dears …. "* "Poor dears." I forced my mind back to the mwores – moors and Meg Merrilies. Now I was to be taught alliteration – whatever that was. I soon came to know and love it. Again I recited:

> "Her apples were swart blackberries,
> Her currants pods o' broom,
> Her wine was the dew of the wild white rose, …. "

"No it was not," she inserted "Her WINE was dew of the WILD HWITE ROSE," "Can't do that," I thought, "hwite is bad enough, without a wild in front of it." In time I conquered that poem, but poor Chalky White never did. My poem describes his efforts.

Chalky White

> Come, Tommy White, and let us see
> If we can teach you how to talk;
> Say, "White, like chalk," but properly,
> Not "chauk," do say it nicely, "chalk."

My mam d' zay I tauks augh right,
An' understan's what I d' zay,
Course I d' knoow that chauk be white,
But dwon'ee teake me vaice away.

It's not your voice that is all wrong,
Your accent "is," note "is," not "be,"
Perhaps we'd better try a song,
You know the tune of "Linden Lea?"

My mam d' tell thick woone t' I,
Ah, reg'lur zhe d' zing'n drough,
I'll come out vront an' 'ave a try;
I knoowed where thick wold woak tree grew.

No doubt you "knew" the "old oak" tree,
And quivered grass-blades under foot.
So, Tommy White has been to see
The woodland and the mossy moot?

Ah, I've a-zid they timber tops,
Beant ne'r a pertier zight t' zee,
Zpied where thick apple be the copse,
Do lean down low in Linden Lea.

"Does," Tommy White, "Does lean down low,"
Tha's what thick apple tree did do –
Oh drat – you've got me at it now;
Class dismiss, for school is drough – through.

Yes, my new teacher was, as I learned later, very "top drawer." She might have been training us to meet royalty. Far fetched? not at all, because a few months later the King and Queen came to stay at the Manor. King George V and Queen Mary, it seemed quite impossible to me. There were pictures of them in the school, there were pictures of them at home, but the real people, here in the village, in their long purple robes with crowns and things, seemed quite out of the question. When they arrived and we were allowed to see them, it was an anti-climax to my dramatic view of the pageantry we were to expect. They were regal, yes, but very – ordinary. Just like the other ladies and gentlemen who went in and out of those wrought iron gates, in, to that splendid place on the other side, or out, to our simple abodes on this side. No fanfares, no processions and nothing that sparkled at all. That is not quite true, the smile of Queen Mary sparkled. She had the charm of a lady who worked in the dairy of Home Farm. If Queen Mary had rolled up her sleeves and begun to wash the **vowls' aggs** (fowls' eggs) for market, I would not have been at all surprised. I had thought the visit might have been more like Empire Day, on 24th May which had been Queen Victoria's birthday; an occasion I did not quite understand, but found exciting.

Empire Day was not a good description, better would have been, Empire Half Day. From noon onwards was a holiday, so every effort was made to speed the proceedings so that all was over when the church clock struck twelve. Thinking back, I have a revulsion for all that surrounded that day, yet at that age the propaganda worked on us all, till we obeyed blindly. Red propaganda, that is what it was. Half the world was red. There was the globe on my teacher's desk, of which she said: "All that is red is the British Empire." In church that morning we sang, *From Greenland's Icy Mountains* and *God bless our Native Land,* an alternative National Anthem. The church service ended with the proper National Anthem – all verses.

That was not the end of the affair, by any means. We then paraded in true military style and marched round the village green, in the centre of which was a flagpole. Round that we marched and formed up in our houses. We saluted, we marched again, we sang endlessly of *The Maple Leaf Forever, Men of Harlech* and various songs describing our greatness. At last came the final salute and the National Anthem, followed by a short pause, I assume for taking in the importance of the occasion. Then came the important part, the half day – yippee!

What was tomorrow and light years away, was there before one could say again *God Bless the Prince of Wales,* and the reply to our teacher's question, "Aren't you proud to be British?" had to be, "Yes, Miss." Pride seemed to be at the centre of most things, but why did she sometimes say to us, "I'm quite ashamed of you.?" Often after saying it she smiled, not unlike Queen Mary smiled. She dressed like her too, with the high-necked collar, with lace across her bosom. Somewhere among those frills was the fine gold chain, at the end of which was a little gold watch. My chief regret in her owning a watch, was that we were never asked to go and find out the time. In the infants' one was asked. A dash into the school yard and a glance at the church clock, then a quick return with, "The big hand's on the three, and the little one's on the twelve." However, I was rarely asked to look at the time, as it took me so very long. Well, if it was sunny there were things to be seen and the warm yard wall was nice to sit on. I enjoyed playing with the little bubbles of tar (pitch) in between the bricks. Then the old gardener needed someone to chat to, a car number to note, and, I must admit, toying with the idea of going home, thinking that I would not be missed. When eventually I arrived back with the time, I got it wrong, could not remember, or got it right, but as so much time had elapsed since my recording, it had become quite useless information.

I hoped for more words that day, words carried emotions, that surely was more important than anything else. The Headmaster was not of the same mind, for with him, first came maths, then history. Maths, dear God, why were they invented? Worse still, if He in His wisdom invented them, why did He also invent those who were good at them? How I detested those who got them right – and so quickly! Occasionally they might have got one wrong. Probably put off by my leaning over to copy. Then of course I got it all wrong as well, in *exactly* the same way.

The Head was one of the hated "get 'em right first timers" and his slickness was quite off-putting. Sometimes he flashed into the room, often disturbing a wonderful story in the writing. "Problem," he would say, and approach the black-board, rubbing off, "I wandered lonely as a cloud." "Problem," he repeated, "If ten boys have twenty oranges and they each cost three farthings, and if five boys eat .... " Oh dear no, how I hated those. Of course most got it wrong – except the hated few. The nastiest bit of the display was the way he showed his working. One line across the middle of the black-board, boys above the line, as with days, price – or even the weather for all I cared! On the bottom went this and that, cancel out, here, here and – here. The answer, two and a half boys! A messy solution which told us nothing. Anyway oranges were not three-farthings and I could have defeated his argument, given a number of oranges to scoff.

He gave me five hundred lines for not paying attention, a fact of which I was quite proud. "I must learn to pay attention in class." This would take one line, and I had become quite adept at holding four pencils between two fingers and could write four lines together in a uniform style. The head soon got to know of my agility and always extended my lines: "I must learn to pay attention in class ..... because ...." Then followed a number of words which defeated my wizardry. On one occasion my mother wrote across my set line and sheets of paper: **"My son will not do lines in his own time."** I handed my powerful reply to the Head. He frowned. "Very well," he said, with a sigh – then gave me the cane.

Doing homework by the light of a large Victorian oil lamp is a pleasant memory. With a huge fire burning in the kitchen range, the room seemed, and still seems warmer than modern rooms, which may be more comfortable, but lack 'something.' It always amazed me, that my father, a farm-labourer, was rather intelligent for his class. He wrote with the most beautiful hand, using exactly the right words – and long ones – composing a letter good enough for the mind of a legal man. I watched the pen move, as smoothly as the river, just beyond the front door, till he signed the bottom, not with a flourish, but in the same rhythmic way. The gift was his. "Why, why," I thought, "is he following a one-share plough pulled by two horses?"

In the science-room were numerous Le Clanché cells being made. The 'wet' battery was only suitable for a doorbell, and as our home had no bell, knocker or letter-box, it was of no use to us. In any case the approach of cottagers in the village, was to open the door and shout, "Anybody home?" If the lady of the house had to be away, a note and/or money would be left for the trader.

Honesty and trust were second nature, so the village policeman was disturbed little from his gardening, bowls, shooting and occasional fishing. His yearly high spot was the supervision of the sheep-dip at the farm. If the bobby approached the farm on other occasions, anyone who saw him might suspect foot and mouth disease on that or some other farm. From adults' expressions I knew that if 'confirmed' it was disasterous. Local louts sometimes caused the policeman problems, as they did when taking his bicycle and hanging it over the river bridge. Why concealing it in that way amused them I shall never know. I do know they laughed for a while at my expense. On their instructons I was sent to the village shop with four farthings, to ask: "A pennyworth of round square ones please," and if there were none, "A penn'th of pigeon's milk." To add to my embarrassment, I asked the lady sitting in the chair on my side of the counter for these strange things. To be redirected and then ridiculed was almost too much for one day.

As a child and perhaps even more so now, if things are being said in whispers, it seems right that the whispers should be louder than, sp–sp–sp. **"It's a case of – you know,"** they lisped. But I didn't know did I? **"Any day they do reckon, an' zhe wonly sixteen."** Even closer one had to be to get the full sound picture. **"Be gone t' ztay wi' her Aunt, they do reckon."** Now I knew what it was all about, who was being discussed, who the Aunt was, what **"You know"** was, in fact I knew more than they did about it all. **"You know"** was a baby, **"Aunt"** was the home the expectant girl had been sent to, where the child would be born and adoption arranged. Dare I tell them who the father was, and worse, he was a distant relative of the girl? It was simply because they were related that I found it quite natural for them to be **"up chalk pit"** disturbing me in my search for precious objects. Perhaps, had I gone earlier to the dump, the event would not have occurred. That is probably a false premise, as things often happen, whatever the circumstances. The Lady of the Manor saw to it that respectability, or rather a facade of it, was retained. Events of this sort were soon forgotten and a 'respectable' marriage arranged. As my father said of these things: **"There 'tis, an' can't be no 'tisser."** and my mother followed with a sigh: **"We mid** [might] **as well zing hymns an' get on wi' it."**

I have now to risk unpopularity, but in a truthful account it is no use glossing over facts. During my school years I hated – nay detested football. Football is a game played by boys trying to be men, or by men attempting to be boys. Somebody has to be impressed by the brute force, the foul, in respect of play or language, or by the dirtiness of the mud on the player's body. Impress the girls, the boys, the non-players or, if those are all who are left, the other players. Most players were quite bearable, it was the hangers-on who, as spectators, refs, judges, experts, or even coroners with their endless post mortems, who drove me from the field to the draughts-board. It was **"Git auff, it was a bleeden mile away y' need glasses,"** and the like, at the Boys second team v Manor staff that appalled me. Two good teams were and are a pleasure to watch, but like the theatre, amateurs can be so very – amateur.

"You don't know what's good for you," they said. I felt then, and still feel that many children do. It was essential to take part in the school sports, even without the slightest hope of a bronze. A gold was for super beings, and on consideration, I am glad I have no gong of precious metal. I believe, had I set out to win, I might have achieved something, but not in the obstacle race. That ended with apple bobbing and the thought of a dozen gasping kids blowing and spitting into a bowl revolted me. I loved sports day in spite of it all. Drinking lemonade, listening, under the beech trees to the sound of the Dorset burr: **"Thick agg be ztuck t' the zpoon."** Achieving nothing but the admiration of my parents.

Wimborne St Giles: almshouse and church

6

"EDIE'S HERE," cried my mother. Looking out of the window, she had spotted Aunt Edith climbing out of a zeppelin. There, through the gap in the hedge, swayed the silver airship, swaying even more as Aunt Edith alighted, removing her flying helmet and goggles. With one final roar of the engine Uncle Fred alighted too. He, unbuttoning his long leather coat with the fur collar. It was a large heavy motor cycle with a square tank and joined to it, still swaying a little, was the silver zeppelin, so fashionable at the time and as 'racy' as Aunt Edith, yet Uncle Fred was not. She was a chain-smoking, chain-swearing, chain-motor cycling addict, and I loved her. Between her bronchial coughing, she greeted all with big hugs, and waited to be asked the first question by my apprehensive mother. **"Edie, isn't it cold on that – machine?"** **"Bugger no,"** gasped Edie, lighting a cigarette. Aunt Edith scattered her swear-words liberally through her conversation. Four letter words may be quite acceptable now, but then such words merely denoted a lack of vocabulary. Aunt Edith's favourite swear-word, delivered with her lovable fruity voice, was more than a four letter word. It was in face, a six letter word. Before too many of these were let loose, we children were bundled out through the back door. **"Dwon't put 'em outzide, 'tis cold as buggery,"** wheezed Aunt Edith.

It made little difference being outside, her voice carried quite well, as if she were an actress playing a role for our benefit. The door might open a little and out would come her hand carrying a bag of sweets. Tousling our heads she might say, **"There y' are, y' greedy little buggers."** Off we went to admire the huge motor cycle. Plenty of others had motor cycles, but few in the village a side-car. Not one had a gleaming silver zeppelin. We were always glad when Aunt Edith came, because that unusual side-car made us a little important for a few hours some Sundays. She, with all her vices, who, so loudly seemed to be accusing the whole world of sodomy and not caring a bugger who heard.

There she was, helping my mother to wash up, smoking, swearing and so – human. My poor mother worried about our sensitive ears and about the best bone china. **"Flora give y' these buggers, didden she?"** **"She did,"** said my mother, taking the plates from her, before she gestured again, or began coughing. She then put them on the dresser, saying, **"Yes, ye'rs ago Flora did."** Now Flora, Edie's and my father's sister, was different. If Edie was chalk, Aunt Flora was certainly cheese.

Aunt Flora lived in a fashionable part of Bournemouth. A large house, or so it seemed, stretched with its vast Edwardian rooms from the front with its spacious sunlit lawn, where they played clock golf, through passages and down little flights of steps to the dark holly and laurel-bushed rear. There were rooms and rooms and still another flight of stairs to the top. There were bedrooms in which no one slept! That seemed to me the height of luxurious waste. In one of those bedrooms was a bed – unslept in – under which was a crocodile. There it was, six feet long, stuffed, lying in wait to frighten, then delight its young visitors. Edith came in a silver zeppelin, but Aunt Flora had a large crocodile under the bed. The trouble was, when I boasted, they just said: **"Pull t'other woone, he got bells on."**

The only problem with Aunt Flora's was in having to behave. Bournemouth is such a wonderful seaside town, it seemed a shame to be enclosed in darkened rooms away from the sun, while the adults talked of rates and the Corporation. I knew little about the latter, except that it appeared on the sides of the trams, all of which seemed to go to Boscombe. In my opinion Aunt Flora's house would have made an excellent museum, but one had to be too careful to *live* there. Apart from Aunt Flora's teaset which adorned our dresser, the nicest things were her parcels at Christmastime. Had Oxfam existed then, she would have run it, giving us first pick. Her parcels gave me the impression we had not eaten, dressed, played, or enjoyed anything at all during the rest of the year.

Parcels seemed to arrive on Boxing Day (there were deliveries that day) and I surmised this was why the day was so named. Postmen made heavy work of it and gained much in the process. By the time the postman reached us he had imbibed a number of **"well, just a half,"** so that **"Ish a bish late to wissh y' a Happy Chrishmash now,"** made little sense to tiny ears. He was invited in for **"jish a liddle"** of dad's parsnip wine, stronger than any wines at the pub and the most potent of my father's collection. "If only people," I thought, "could be as happy, as generous and as loving as they are now, wouldn't the world be a lovely place?"

My thoughts turn to less happy times. Most families have rows. A clash of wills, a misunderstanding and a heated argument occurs. However, bitterness, real bitterness is something the child should be shielded from. Surely wild abuse and exposure of sordid details are not good for a child, surely it undermines his security? Money, or lack of it caused many of such rows, and they developed into fierce battles. I waited for the dreaded finale from my mother: **"I shall run away vrom it all."** "Dear God no, what would we do?" I thought. **"Fine,"** from my father. **"No mam, no,"** from me. **"Goo on out t' play,"** shouted my mother. "Go out to play at a time like this?" Indeed yes, for the child learns that much of the drama is produced for effect. I came to know as many a policeman has, family rows should be left to subside.

Back to the class-room and Class 2, back to the high-windowed Victorian prison, but back to words and music. I bore geography with all its silly place names. Does it matter where places are, unless one is going to them, just passing, or leaving? From the description of some of them, the latter might be the best alternative. Now, geography transformed into words is something which interested me. Better still transformed into an aide memoir: "Great big Italy kicked poor Sicily into the Mediterranean Sea." it had humour, it was a clever use of words, and it made things more interesting; that was the important point.

History had dates and people concerned with dates. I did not care to memorize dates, no more than I tried to remember where Malaya was, though I wish I had, for I was to be there a few years later. I did not care how many wives Henry VIII had, why he had them, which followed who, or who preceded which. I had to accept he got rid of them, how, when and why held no interest for me. He did not seem to be a very attractive person and did appear to do exactly as he wished, the very thing we were being advised against. History was very dry when presented as lists of people or dates to be remembered. It was not all like that, there was real history in that part of Dorset. On the downs surrounding the village, there were tumili, the Bronze Age burial mounds. Long barrows and round were excavated by General Pitt Rivers and all those precious finds taken to his home and museum

Rows and rows of stones, that is what it appeared to be. Stones of different shapes, stones that were axe-heads, stones that were chipped away, but incomplete as instruments and unexplained stones. There was pottery that had been found near those sitting ancient men in their graves, which held the food for their 'new lives,' and pieces of pottery, from large chunks to tiny fragments. To Pitt Rivers each piece meant a great deal, as they have to so many down the years. I knew that Dorset boasted many great men and that General Pitt Rivers was among them. I am grateful that many a history lesson was spent in his museum. Things – real things – are so much better for the imagination than pictures. Some of Pitt Rivers collection is now in London, but the bulk is at Oxford or Salisbury.

"Wonderful," I thought, **"Delicious,"** my mother would have said of those Sundays spent near the museum. I say near, quite deliberately. Near the museum was the Larmer Tree, and behind it the Larmer Grounds. Fantasy intrigues most people, and my childhood was wrapped in it, and, alas from that point of view I never grew up. The Larmer Grounds were pure fantasy and like many things, difficult to describe, they must be experienced.

Imagine then a hot sunny Sunday afternoon. A field with its grass mown to perfection, on which a languid game of cricket is being played. Brown arms of white-clad cricketers, the pink, and getting pinker arms of summer-dressed ladies. Ladies looking cool in spite of the sun, men looking hot because of it, or just to impress. A brass band playing under the awning and the general sleepy – nothing matters – English feeling of it all. Gaze at the Larmer Tree, chained around the trunk to help preserve it. Then wander towards the turnstile and come back with me in time to one of the most pleasant mysteries of my childhood.

From the strong sunlight to the cool shadow of exotic trees, almost as close-planted as the jungle. Leaving behind the restraints of a puritanical Dorset Sunday, strip your mind of nicely polished shoes and pressed clothes. Leave your family and its Bible and search for the Koran, for there must be a copy here. Leave Evensong, leave *Abide with Me,* and venture into the world of the East. Deeper into the undergrowth, down to limpid pools, where you may startle and be startled by exotic birds. Look this way, peer that, and find something different, something enchanting at every glance. **"Do all zeem ztrange,"** strange yet compelling. This is the dream, this might even be the nightmare, but it is compelling.

An eastern straw temple, looking like a series of beehives, starting from large and ascending to, in fact, a beehive, for there are bees entering and departing at its summit. Still looking up, yet seeing none of the Dorset sky, take in with some disbelief, the pagoda amid the palms. This cannot be Dorset, this Utopia, yet surrounded by little Dorset villages. This is some wild stretch of the imagination, out of which we must come with a rude awakening by the **"Howzat?"** cry from some other world. I invited you to come with me, but for a while we should part within this eastern paradise. Each to his own temple, so that in time to come we still have the utter serenity of this divine place. We may each look back and say in our own way: "I remember," and continue with the lines of the popular song of the day, *This is my lovely day, this is the day I shall remember the day I am dying, they can't take this away ....*

We must go back to the class-room, to my abhorrence of geography, my love-hate relationship with history and to the pure love of words and music. No doubt I was told at that time, by teachers and others, that a number of subjects are so dependent on each other, as at times to be inseparable. I was told and there is little doubt that at that time I was dreaming.

In the production of school plays I came to know some very basic rules. Low sounds suggest sadness and higher sounds turn the mind towards gladness. I also saw that from the dramatic point of view, and in simple terms, movement descends with a low sound and ascends as the sound rises. From the rule-of-thumb guide came some understanding of nature, the feel, the sight and the sound of it. It gave me the desire to go deeper into the mystery of drama, which must be only a reflection of life. I am eternally grateful to the little village school for giving me my first words and music and must thank someone that the school was set in a Dorset village, where my knowledge of standard English grew with the love of my native Dorset dialect. I cannot *feel* my roots in the sound, that was popularly called an "Oxford" accent.

From words to movement and to dancing. Dancing, like talking is within each person, I discovered. Some did both well, while others barely moved a tongue or foot in the right direction. At dancing I was a slow starter, but once my feet had stepped this way or that to a particular rhythm, they were itching to go, as soon as "Butterfly" or "Durham Reel" was mentioned. One or two of the better dancers in the school scoffed at my slippers, several sizes too big and kept on with elastic around my insteps. I knew embarrassment, dancing in my pale-blue satin-faced slippers, but soon lost it, as with my partner Peggy, I became one of the better performers in country dancing. However, as fits my pattern, my praise was overshadowed by condemnation. When the music and dance teacher mentioned my ability to the Head, she said: "Jimmy is so light on his feet." He replied crisply: "He is the other end too," as he walked off to some other part of the school.

I forgave his sarcasm because he had made good use of words and because he knew about poetry, being an admirer of Hardy. Hardy spent a great deal of his time in London, as have I, but William Barnes, the great Dorset dialect poet, rarely left the county. His writing was not contrived "away from the scene." He lived and felt his poems, almost as part of the countryside himself. I read more deeply and came to understand that my teacher was wrong; there was no shame in the accent or dialect, no more than there was shame in sex, poverty, or being different from the accepted norm. I loved the sound of village people and today feel much better when asked: **"How do, an' how bist?"** than: "Good afternoon, and how are you?" I cannot remember the "voices and faces of that place," but can bring to mind, the **"vaices an' feäces o' thick pleäce."** William Barnes told Dorset people not to be ashamed. I never have been, and my poems show I never shall despise my Dorset origins. Simple beginnings have great advantages, and "simple" should never be confused with stupid.

So began my exploration of words and music. Words are capable of being picked up, but music is born in the child. It was with a sense of shock that I learned of Mozart writing his first piece at the age of seven – my age. "Mozart and great music were very far from the school," I thought, yet great music had been composed in the village. Handel, sitting a few yards from where I sat, wrote part of his *Messiah*. I liked to think that the village and countryside inspired him and that, as the great composer, I might in my way, be inspired. I roamed the downs, writing little verses, which later became poems. I stored away in my mind the beauty of the countryside and the Dorset dialect and set them into poems as I grew older.

Standard 2 of the village school did not aim towards the heights of Handel or Mozart, but the National Song Book was a good start. The new song to be learnt was written on a sheet of paper, then copies made on a 'jelly.' The image was transferred to the surface of the jelly, then about fifty copies were made, by pressing, rubbing and peeling them off. The last few were barely readable. Having promised myself to be an actor, I needed the sheet for a very short time. I had begun the business of remembering lines. Many of the songs had funny choruses, which had to be sung with gusto. One of those tongue-twisters went like this:

> "Hi diddle um cum, tar un tantum,
> Through the town of Ramsay,
> Hi diddle um cum over the lea,
> Hi diddle um cum feedle."   .... Whatever all that meant.

Barbara Allen, now that was more like it. Sad, but at least it told a story which played on the emotion. That song was, and is worth careful study. It is pure melodrama, but the story can be related to every-day life. Here was a young maiden, visiting Jemmy Grove, her lover. (so we assume) He is on his death-bed 'for love of her.' Her 'change of heart' is so well conveyed in this verse of the song:

> "Then slowly slowly she came up,
> And slowly she came nigh him,
> And all she said when there she came;

[Now comes the crunch. To be sung without emotion, each word measured out as rapid machine-gun fire.]

> Young man, I think you're dying."

She, however, goes on to break her own heart, because of **"the fault she fell in,"** in being so very hard. Bidding her farewells, as do the great operatic sopranos, she begs her mother make her bed, on which she prepares to die, tomorrow.

Fifehead Magdalen

7

LIFE AND work on and around the farm was in those days tough for men, and not exactly easy for women, who often went to work in the fields, after attending to their housework, the children and shopping. Shopping was for emergency supplies only, as grocers, bakers, butchers, and many other suppliers called with vans, taking orders and delivering a few days later. The problem with having things delivered, was that the trader often left unsatisfactory goods. There was a baker, for instance, who had a poor reputation in his cake-making. His currant buns were not too aptly named, for they contained few currants. **"Tell 'ee what,"** my father would complain, **"I reckon 'ee do goo up top o' hill an' zhoot they currants in wi' a catteepolt** [catapult]. To which my mother nodded assent, adding, **"'Zpect 'ee do."** A pause, during which my father might sigh before he said: **"I'll tell 'ee zummit else,"** and continue with conviction, **"He be a bloody rotten zhot."**

The work of a farm–labourer's wife was almost unending. Harvest time was the busiest, when the mother with her children 'took in' a field of corn which had been cut by the binder, the sheaves lying in neat rows. It needs to be said that the fields of Dorset were large, many the size of a farm in some parts of the country. That field of corn, newly cut, may have been between thirty and fifty acres. With sheaves almost as far as the eye could see, there had to be a lot of fetching and carrying before the field was **hiled. Hiling** was the standing of the sheaves upright in stooks, which were called **hiles.** These were left to dry in the sun for a week or so, when a cart would **car** [carry] the sheaves load by load to make a rick in a corner of the field. When all the corn was **carr'd** [carried], the ricks were thatched and during the winter the threshing done. Had you been there and asked for the farmer, you might have been told: **"He'm carren vifty eacres."** [He is carrying corn sheaves in the fifty acre field]. Hiling the sheaves was tough on little hands and thirsty work too, so bottles of cold tea would be left in the shade of the hedge or nearby trees. By the same shade one of the children may have been left to watch the pram containing the youngest member of the family, with a large umbrella acting as a sunshade and instructions to shush the flies. They might gather on a hot day, attracted by the workers' dinner which could be stowed in the pram. No five-star fare, but bread with the rabbit from rabbit stew, washed down by tea, was welcome to the family group, who were glad **"vor a bit o' rest in the zheade."** The rabbit for the meal may well have been caught the day before.

I was seven when I 'caught' my first rabbit. The binder had cut the corn down to a tiny triangle and there, cowering in the last few stalks, was 'my' rabbit. Mine, because it was my initiation to the ritual killing of something which had no hope of escape. I had to take a stick and beat the rabbit's head, as those around cried, **"Go on Jimmy, this woone's thine."** That one was indeed mine, and it is with shame that I admit it. Not all in the countryside is pretty.

To err is human, how I erred, and still do. If it was possible for something to be made wrongly, said wrongly, or even rightly, but still seeming wrong, then it would be made, said, or in some way contrived by me. The class-rooms were all spick and span, as were teachers and pupils. Faces shone, hair shone, desks shone, even the sun shone on, surely the nearest perfection has ever known within a little country school. The School-Inspector was coming, as his title suggested, to inspect the school. We had been drilled down to the last detail, well, almost the last. "You must answer promptly," we had been told, "Any question he may ask." I practised with myself, playing both parts and did very well indeed. "How old are you? How tall are you? Where do you live? Oh yes, I could have no difficulty with any of his silly questions." As they say today, "Wanna bet?"

He arrived amid the silence that usually precedes a storm. All the teachers were as some other beings and sounding so much more educated than they could possibly have been. As being at the dentist, it is the waiting not the tooth which is intolerable. Still we waited, till I felt and must have looked like a little misshapen statue. I would have given all I had for a mug of water, for I was quite sure my mouth was too dry to allow any words to come out. At last he reached us, just at the moment when least expected. Of course I was almost last to be questioned, and even then it seemed like an afterthought, as he delivered his boomerang. Putting one hand on my desk and leaning forward, with what I swear was a leer, he rapped out: "Why do I wear spectacles?" I pulled the trigger and fired back, almost before his missile reached me. "Because you can't see, Sir." I knew when only half way through that I was wrong, but worse, I suspect they all knew before I replied that I would get it wrong. My teacher looked to high Heaven, and, behind his back, sighed with resignation. She smiled sweetly as he turned to her and he beamed back, then at the class, saying: "Because ....?" "Because they help you to see better," came the chorus of starling-like replies, while I would have been grateful for the air-gun I had been shown the day before, with which I would gladly have picked them off one by one.

There is a great deal of unfairness in life, and so much of it was packed into my days at school. My mind went blank at the sight or sound of anything I found uninteresting. It is a useful escape from a lot of things, but it is the only way out of a difficult maths question. Exams, and the blank sheets to be filled with answers, came round all too often. Those maths problems which came in so many parts, did try my patience, so I simply wrote against the question, "This one is impossible to answer." It added little to my exam results, or to my popularity.

So I turned to music for solace. Music comes in so many forms and one note, even a suggested note could strike a whole chord. A complete summer symphony could have been set to the sounds of bleating sheep with their rattling tinny bells as they munched the grass out on the downs. Whilst lying, gazing into the sky, the sound of soaring skylarks, zimmering – if there is such a word – dragon-flies and the distant sound of church bells augmented my orchestra. School music was very clinical, as children were not reckoned to have a high emotional reaction to such an art form. I believe their reckoning was wrong in some cases.

In the music room, class reared its ugly head. There were the gifted ones called "sight readers," said in hushed tones, I assumed because they were so clever. Among the select few were a number who were allowed to sing parts. We poor melody singers just waited around while the chosen few grasped their parts. Long before they had achieved this, I knew all the parts and when it came to the grande ensemble, sang which ever part suited my mood. Imitating one or two of the sight readers who sang 'carefully' added pleasure to the situation.

English often followed music and I went to it with eagerness. The technical part, like construction, sent me to sleep. Had I stayed awake, I might have done better in the essay which followed. One standard text book appealed to me, as it

had been compiled by someone with a sense of humour. Answer the following:
The boy went into the shop to buy some ......

Airships
Houses
Trees
Children
Sweets

Early in the book the answers were as obvious as the above, but later the questions became more difficult. A great thrill for me, was finding an answer to:
England has a very ..... population. Among the words was 'dense.' Not only did I know the word, but I also spotted the pun. It pleased my teacher, and, as a result, me.

My teacher's dinner [lunch] was served at her desk. Her husband, the organist, brought it to her, steaming hot and covered by a damask snow-white cloth, together with a similar napkin. With the silver cutlery laid out on her desk, she ate with grace, as if she were at Claridges at least. Occasionally she dabbed the corner of her mouth with the napkin, and looked at us over the top of her gold-rimmed spectacles, as we munched our way through soggy sandwiches at speed, a game of rounders taking preference over dinner, which was not unlike a religious ritual.

Children have always enjoyed playing or experimenting with words. One boy in my class, whom I admired greatly, though he was apt to be sacrilegious, followed in the steps of Doctor Spooner. "All things beaut and brightiful," he sang at prayers. He sang with delight as I stood on one of his toes, as if it was the soft-pedal of an organ. His singing grew louder, as I trod down on the brake of his singing vehicle, now almost out of control and hurtling beyond reason downhill. Hands together, I pleaded, "Please let the singing stop before he gets into trouble." It stopped, but then began the Lord's Prayer. The altered words that followed do not bear repeating. Perhaps I found his little song more amusing. Its last line was as follows: "For if you play with a *bee baw bum* you're sure to get a sting." That was one of his better reversals.

Music lingers in the mind, that is why it is so important. One of my early school memories was the Grace before dinner, set to the *Old Hundredth:*

"Be present at our table Lord,
Be here and everywhere adored,
These creatures bless and grant that we
May feast in paradise with Thee."

"That is the same as 'All people that on earth do dwell,'" I told my teacher. She beamed and agreed, and I beamed back with some satisfaction. By now it will be apparent I was not a complete success at school. Then, as now, I had a way of cancelling one success with a complete disaster. So the setting of that hymn tune and my knowledge of it, was ruled out when I asked: "Please Miss, what do I do when I ander?" She was greatly perplexed. We had learnt the song *The Ash Grove* and a line puzzled me. "Well Miss," I said, "Down yonder green valley where stream lets me ander." She was at first amused, then said: "You're stupid, what are you?" "Stupid Miss," I replied, still anxious for some explanation. "Your mind meanders," she said, "Where streamlets meander," she said forcibly. "Thank you Miss," I replied, all the time thinking, why don't grown-ups think of childrens' vocabularies when writing? After all, I went to church for my first year at school thinking militant meant being gentle, "militant here on earth," I simply associated it with mild. Perhaps I was lazy? Indeed I know I was. My father said, "What is the dictionary for?" I explained that it was sometimes difficult to find a word if I did not know its spelling. He had no suitable answer, and I still have the problem.

"So, what on earth will you be when you grow up?" they said. "An actor," I replied. "Not with a name like James Attwell," they scoffed, which made me more determined to act or write under the name I was born with. "A name needs a ring to it," they persisted, "that's what you need." "Something with a ring to it," I thought. The village had that in its church, the finest peal for miles. My name took second place to the title of my next poem.

Village Bells

I d' yer 'em Zunday marnen,
   A-ringen out across the downs,
Pealen o' their Christian warnen,
   An' they d' meake the zweetest zoun's.

They d' meake the zunshine warmer,
   Meake 'ee veel all good inzide;
Breaks the zet-veace o' the varmer,
   Turns winter int-a Eastertide.

Up the valley comes the ringen,
   The wind a-teaken it along,
Pitched like tunen varks vur zingen,
   An' matchen o' the blackbird's zong.

I d' zee the hair-bells blowen,
   An' yer the zkylark out o' zight,
Wi' the zummer colours glowen,
   Veel all tha's in God's world be right.

An' the river all a-glimmer,
   As if revlecten o' the peal,
Heat-haze meakes the zky a-zhimmer,
   Like zome girt back-cloth that beant real.

Wi' the zoun' o' zheep bells clanken,
   As if to answer o' the chime;
In me mind I got t' thank'n,
   Vur zight, vur zoun', vur zummertime.

Thoogh girt cathedral bells mid zoun'
   Vur some good vo'k, I 'ould tell they,
That I dwon't envy o' the town,
   Thick village bells calls I t' pray.

"**Tis gitten on vur Christmas,**" said my father and mother in turn. Getting on for, it was miles away. The pile of parcels on the top of the kitchen dresser was getting taller each week after their visit to Salisbury. I supposed it was connected with Christmas, because when Christmas Eve eventually came and all the rustling and whispering began: "**That one in there, no his, ah, sh, now this** ...." and Christmas morning came [5 am] the dresser top was clean and bare.

"**How about the zweep?** [sweep]," they said, "**Better have the zweep jist avore Christmas,**" and continued, "**Ah, Christmas Eve is best vur it, the zitten—room.**" "No," I thought, "dirty brushes and the mess of soot, with all those lovely things around, that would be terrible. The sweep was needed before the preparations for this great festival began." Every time the subject arose things were written on small pieces of paper. The whole idea worried me and I felt quite sure Christmas would be ruined. It was much nearer the time of celebration when I came to know that the sweep was a silly old game grown-ups played.

The charm of Christmas was more evident in that part of the country and I feel sure it meant more at that time because of the very word, Christmas. Everybody seemed more aware of it, and although a great deal of the pagan festival was there, a baby in a manger who came to earth as God, was the thought uppermost in people's minds. Christmas carols were known by heart in their entirety and carollers sang several at each house, then the group could be invited in for mince pies, hot drinks and oranges. I have never felt closer to Christmas – the real Christmas – than when singing carols outside the warmly-lit windows of those Dorset cottages. "Still the night, Holy the night," we sang, and within the silence and stillness of the village, our voices were the only sound to be heard. We were welcomed by all and asked to sing "**Jist woone mwore.**" Welcomed by all? there was an exception.

The dear lady at the little lodge by the Manor's main gate will go down in my history and that of many others for a classic remark. The carol singers had sung at her door and shortly after, the handbell ringers with their mellow sounds rang a selection for her. A brief spell and the village band played yet more carols near her door. No sooner had they begun to play, than the door was flung open and her obvious fury stopped them mid tune. With arms akimbo, she groaned: "**First the singers, then the ringers and now the buggering band.**" Like my Aunt Edith, her vocabulary was extensive. So near to Christmas and in such close proximity to the church was shocking enough to bear repeating. I do so now because of my love of things said – and said to be remembered.

Wimborne Minster

8

CHRISTMAS, SO longed for in its advent, yet in a twinkling, over, or almost over. There was still in early January, the Childrens' Christmas party. Held in the school, it was something we arrived for very early. Part of the fascination was watching the preparations. The tall Christmas tree with its candles being lit with a long taper, a mass of coloured candles, reflecting one by one, bringing life, colour and sparkle to the tree, with its superb decorations. I say superb, because they and the tree were supplied each year by the Lady of the Manor. Many of the ornaments on the tree were the old German ones, fine in design and in their subdued but rich stained-glass colours. There we waited with noses pressed to the cookery-room window, as the stoves with their many kettles, augmented by things from the Manor's kitchen, steamed into action, filling large dark glazed teapots, teapots that needed both hands for carrying and manipulation. That it was cold outside was of no consequence, for inside was all the splendour and promise of a near-to-Heaven experience.

At last the door was opened and the rush to be nearest the best cakes began. Rather like musical chairs, the slightest hesitation and one's position was lost. Cakes as far as the eye could see, many more than could be taken in at a glance, many more than could be grasped in many glances. Plates and plates of *thin* bread and butter, both white and brown. Several of those tiny thin triangles could be scoffed in one swoop, while the Housekeeper from the Manor, over one's right shoulder asked: "More tea?" How could one reply with all the cramming that had to be done? A nod seemed sufficient, and from the large shining teapot into one's cup – and all the cups and saucers matched – came yet more tea, and the almost silent eating continued, as if we had not eaten for a long time.

There was nothing on that table, though it groaned under the weight, that we could not have had at home. It was the setting-out, the vast amount, the colour and the excitement which made it all so different. There was something else that was different too, the presents. The Lady of the Manor joined the party when most of the serious eating had been done, though there was still room for one of those little round ones with jam spread on, which was covered with coconut. Just room enough for one more before her Ladyship began: "Good afternoon children … " Then home to my mother's remark: **"You woon't want nothen t' eat vur a wick** [week] **now."** "No," I squeezed out, but doubted the truth of it.

A cold and wet January morning was not the best of times to walk two miles to school. The first day of term, walking, wet and for the first time, with my little sister Iris, to be taken to the infants' class. She was a frail creature, small limbed, pale and delicate, and I held her little hand tightly, or surely the wind might have whisked her away. I was responsible, so could not make the excuse, "Mam, the wind took her away," and then assure my father (she was his favourite) that she would be back. I delivered her to the infants' room where I was convinced she would collapse. I told her I would be back at break-time, for I had firm instructions to give her a fairy cake – and to see that she ate it. These fairy cakes were actually the tiny sponge cakes used for making trifles. My thoughts were not with my own class for that first day.

Perhaps my gran should have taken the blame for all the fear on my sister's behalf. When Iris was a baby, gran had said to my mother: **"Blue veined she is,**

when they'm blue veined, they dwon't live." True Iris had a blue vein in her forehead, but she is alive and happy fifty years on from that remark. Iris soon took to school and my fears were unfounded. She soon appeared to be as tough as most of the girls, and for that matter, the boys. My first wrong assumption of the weaker sex? For all that, I still feel I want to cry when I see those little sponge cakes. I was glad when my mother came to collect her in the afternoon – no, I was not glad, again it was embarrassing.

Many of the cottagers went **'ooden** [wooding], collecting fire-wood from the woods surrounding the village. With a hand-cart, or in our case an old pram, women trundled across the park to collect their kindling-wood. That they should do this I did not mind, but calling at school on the way back, the old pram loaded to capacity, was just a little humiliating. **"Tell Iris her mam is yer,"** my mother **hawked** [yelled] to someone in the yard. "Who is that shouting?" my teacher asked, in a perfectly modulated voice. "Jimmy's mum," at least three of my 'friends' chorused, while I tried to hide my face from the scorn of the children who were fortunate enough to have mothers who waited for them to come home. If the weather was stormy, I awaited the next shout: **"Tell Jim too, 'cos 'tis gwoen t' rain."** I got out quickly and hurried away with my sister, both of us holding the handle of the pram, my mother still shouting back to one of the teachers: **"'Tis gwoen t' thunder I 'zpect, I zhould let 'em all goo hwome now, 'vore do come on heavy."** From me, in a hoarse whisper came: "Come on mam." No pausing to investigate things on this journey home, not even a moment to listen to a strange bird, or to the singing of the telegraph wires. **"We must hurry,"** urged my mother, **"We must git hwome an' cover up the looken-glasses, 'vore do come on too heavy, an' wopen all the doors."** Covering the mirrors had some logic as they might seemingly attract lightning, but opening doors was **"to let it out"** – the thunder! This was probably based on the idea that if a thunder-bolt came down the chimney, it would roll out of the door.

"Next Zunday," said my father, **"we'm gwoen t' zee Aunt Bessie,"** That was very good news. Aunt Bessie, my father's sister, was a buxom, round and jolly woman. She was always huggable and loved children. Her cottage was a few villages away and half way to Blandford, which meant an exciting bus ride along the main road to a point where she met us. Aunt Bessie had a gramophone, a big square wooden thing, with a massive horn. She had a good number of records too, and though many were of brass bands playing military marches, there was one record which was our 'No. 1.' **"Dwon't 'ee dare play that one,"** she pleaded. "Please, please, please," we yelled. **"Well then, you must close the doors and windows,"** she whispered, **"Vor if the policeman do hear, I zhall be put in jail."** The record in question was *Aint it Grand to be Bloomen well dead*. It was a 'banned' record, a rare thing for the period, but the ban was probably placed on it to discourage sales. In retrospect it was harmless, but at the time quite shocking and therefore exciting and compulsive listening:

> "Look at the coffin, bloomen great handles,
> Aint it grand to be bloomen well dead,
>
> Look at the bearers, bloomen great hats on,
> Aint it grand to be bloomen well dead" … and so on.

In later years Aunt Bessie gave us her gramophone and piles of her records, but not that one. Perhaps we were denied that in respect for the dead.

I have said before that death plays an important part in a child's growing up. Indeed death must be respected at all levels. There was in the village, I thought, an absurd position regarding death and the ritual that surrounded it. Coffins were made by the local carpenter who was also the blacksmith. There was sadness as he performed the last task for a villager, mourning the passing of a friend.

On the other side of the village was a small holding, a house with a shed and a stable, in which was a black horse. Alongside was the shed in which were two carts. One of these was not for the fields and muddy lanes, it was in fact the bier. A solemn looking vehicle, a leftover from the Victorian era, it made the half-mile journey between the church and cemetery. Led by the priest and followed by the mourners, the black-clad stream moved up the hill, in silence, apart from the clip-clop of the horse's hooves and the trundling of the cart. This could have been a Friday, but my real observation is concerned with Saturday, Saturday in the shooting season.

At the end of the procession of shooters and beaters, came the same horse pulling the same sort of cart, except that now the cart carried a series of dead bodies. On view, dangling and swinging as the cart rocked on its journey. Solemn and upright the farmer led his horse, with due reverence for all the bodies in his charge. No flowers on the top of this vehicle. Did no one care, or was it too sudden? Half expecting braces of pheasants to be walking behind the cart, I watched. Who was to tell the difference, as the farmer looked much the same as the day before, except he had no top hat and black crepe? A painter, perhaps of the impressionist school, might have painted the absurdity I saw. The horse stopped, knowing its destination in front of the church, where after a pause, the West door opened. The verger came down the steps to greet the cortége, then opening the wrought iron gates by his lodge, allowed the solemn procession to pass through to the Manor and the deceaseds' final resting place.

The Lodge gates were the main ones and those most used for entry to the Manor. There were other gates across the park, the furthest being a mile from the village. At the main gates a number of villagers had gathered. Today the Duchess of Kent [Princess Marina] was to arrive for a stay at the Manor. **"Bee 'ee comen down t' zee her?"** they asked my mother. **"Lard noo, I be gooen 'ooden,"** [wooding] she replied, then added, **"Royalty woon't git me vire gooen, will 'em?"** It might be assumed from this that she had no interest in them. The reverse was true, she not only admired them, but almost considered them part of her family. **"Zhe was a Bowes-Lyon before she married,"** [Queen Elizabeth the Queen Mother] she might remark, and add, **"We'm the zame age y' know."** However, she was not going to wait at the main gates to see Princess Marina arrive. **"I like her, mind you an' I like the colour named atter her,"** [Marina green] **"But I beant weaten aroun' vor her,"** and off she went with her old pram to the park and the beech trees, where there would be plenty of dry wood.

The knot of people at the main gate waited a very long time, during which my mother was loading up with fallen beech limbs. Half way along one of the gravel drives in the park she saw approaching a procession of cars. In a Rolls was Princess Marina, who instructed the driver to stop, and with the window wound down, my mother having done her, 'bob' as she called it, the Princess chatted to her about the park and the village, then with another 'bob' from my mother, she continued to the front door of the Manor. The gleam in my mother's eye might have suggested she was privy to the information on the route of visiting royalty, as she strutted with her pram-load of wood, back through the village, pausing with great pride to announce at the main gate: **"Zhe 'm already arrived,"** and striding off home with her **"two birds with woone ztwone,"** expression.

From the Rolls Royce entering the Manor grounds my memory travels to the Ford parked at the back of the farm buildings. When I say parked, I really mean stationary, in fact it had been static for many a year. Grass grew over what remained of its springs, the wheels having been removed some years before, which made little difference to the trips we made. We took it in turns to drive, by we I mean several boys from the village who were car-minded. Non car-people were not allowed in the front seats, which were rusted brackets, where once fine leather had rested. There was a great deal of lime on, in and under our car. Lime, not from the chalk fields around, but from the droppings of the chickens who used the vehicle when it was not out on hire to us. We had to attend many weddings in our car, in fact we always seemed to be on the way to, or returning from a wedding. Like a badly written, or badly set play, we were unable to move the action from the car, that is except in the preparations for the reception, and that was held a few feet from the car where the broken wind-screen lay.

If I remember the plot correctly, our plates, which were pieces of glass from the wind-screen, were placed near a stone circle, which was a secure base for our fireplace. On a piece of tin we were to fry pheasants eggs which we had taken from a nest in the long grass – it is too late for the gamekeeper to act now. There was never a bride or bridegroom in our play, all that, was 'off stage,' and I believe the 'trip' by car was just an excuse to attend the reception, which was just about to begin. On this occasion I was with three other boys in the back of the wedding car, when, looking through the small oval window at the rear, we saw a lad standing on the ridge above the yard. We called him names from the safety of our 'speeding' car, till, annoyed, he picked up a handful of stones and began to aim them at our oval rear window, most of them missing. The art was to peer through the window and as a stone came, bob down. This action continued till, in my usual vein, I bobbed up as the others bobbed down. It was at that precise moment when he scored a direct hit, shattering the window and catching my mouth with the glass, resulting in a cut lip and the cancellation of the reception. The other boys took me to a, not too clean, cattle trough, half filled with dirty water, to administer first aid. Said one boy: **"Yur lip do need a cobweb,"** and I went home for the treatment.

Cobwebs gathering dust in a corner do not seem the best thing to apply to open wounds. It was a method of treatment with country people and it would stop bleeding, as it did in this case. Had it been a sting from ants or a nettle, no doubt a dock leaf would have been applied, or for ear-ache, a small shallot in the ear. For aches and pains in the limbs a potato might have been carried in the pocket, for a headache, some elder flower tea, and for a cold, onion broth. Jack and Jill's vinegar and brown paper was not too odd. Brown paper and goose grease was used for chest colds.

Not all my play was as dangerous as my 'car accident.' Much of my play was solitary. At the time when I first came to know William Barnes's *My Orcha'd in*

Linden Lea, I realized he had drawn his picture from life – it could have been mine. Every word in his poem has the ring of truth and made a great impression on me.

> "'Ithin the woodlands, flow'ry gleaded,
>   By the woak tree's mossy moot,
> The sheenen grass-bleades, timber sheaded,
>   Now do quiver under voot;
> An' birds do whissle over head,
> An' water's bubblen in its bed,
> An' there vor me the apple tree
> Do lean down low in Linden Lea."

I have travelled a great deal since coming to those words, and have always been glad to come back to my village, which was and is my 'Linden Lea.' His fine words have so often sped my return

> "... I be free to goo abrode,
> Or teake agean my hwomeward road
> To where, vor me, the apple tree
> Do lean down low in Linden Lea."

"Vine words," my father said, **"But 'tis actions we need,"** echoed my mother. They were referring to a candidate in an election. Sir So and So for the Conservatives, Mr. Such and Such for the Liberals and Jack – or some other ordinary name – for Labour. They spoke of Labour and not Socialism. Candidates called at each house appealing for votes and offering so many things, among which was a lift by car to the polling station. My mother, with her usual gleam in her eyes, went in a car sporting a Tory rosette – she and the car! On entering the school yard and the polling station, some onlooker was bound to say to her: **"Mind 'ee do put yer cross in the right pleace."** **"Ah, I zhall,"** she replied, but her decision was known only to her. I never was sure of her political leanings, I can only recall her remark: **"Thees can lead a hoss t' water, but thees cassen meake'n drink."**

She said almost as little about voting, as Joe, who lived at a nearby farm, of his romance. He met a girl and took her for a Sunday walk. They walked alongside each other, but apart, for some miles. Along the turnpike, through the woods, over the downs and finally back down the hill to her home. Not a word was spoken till their parting, when Joe drew a deep breath and said: **"I'm gooen dung zpreaden t'mar"** [tomorrow].

**Wimborne: Julian's Bridge
over the Stour**

9

FOOD PLAYS an important part in children's lives. Quite often my play was divided between particular things to be eaten. Lunch, dinner, tea, or supper did not apply, **"We're gwoen t' have rhubarb pudden,"** did. New bread, direct from the bakery is a memory dear to many, and, seeing TV advertisements for bread, set in the good old-fashioned way, I believe I might have been a good model for such an ad. I must first explain the cottage loaf. The bottom was a circular loaf itself and it was topped with a smaller round loaf. When baked, the top was often browner than the bottom and had a crustiness not known in modern bread. Add to that a good hunk of cheese – Cheddar, we knew no other – plus some pickled onions and the combination is almost too mouth-watering to describe. I longed to be called to, **"Goo an' git a lwoaf."** I went eagerly to the bakery, collected the loaf and made a slow journey home. On arrival my mother took the loaf and removed the top. **"Yes, I thought so,"** she observed, **"You bin at'n."** I had indeed been at him [it]. Removal of its topknot revealed a most tender piece of loaf at its softest just where it joined the base. Newly baked, that part was delicious. Oh yes, there was a hole where there should have been bread, but the slap did not outweigh the pleasure of **"the best bit o' the lwoaf."**

Next to new bread came slab cake, which I must also attempt to describe. Imagine a rich Dundee cake, with much more fruit, but less nuts, and you will have an idea. Square, deeper and darker than the Dundee cake, it came in large pieces – slabs – hence its name. The cottage loaf and slab cake came from the same bakery. The Baker was a kindly man with large brown eyes. I do not know why, but I shall always associate his brown-eyed smile with slab cake. Association of ideas perhaps, if that is so, then our film shows must be linked in the same way. He brought pleasure to the village with a film once a week. His projector set up in the village hall, we sat through many wonderful films on the small screen. We also sat through many intervals. Suddenly at the climax of a scene, came XXXX 1111 or 2222, then a series of unreadable things and finally a blinding white light, and with many "Oh's" we waited for the next reel. Sometimes the sound broke down and that meant a longer wait. Our baker with his large smiling brown eyes, brought us good bread, slab cake and films. All that pleasure was, and is one to me, and contained within the warmth of a smile.

High tea is another relic of the Edwardian age. High tea is of course a combination of tea and supper, the tea-y things with something cooked. One of the bigger boys with whom I played, got a little cross when his parents invited me in for high tea, simply because I was well behaved – in their house. In my own environment I was what is called, uncontrollable. We sat down for the meal, a large family around a large table. Perhaps this was the meal we would enjoy and not be worried too much by their big joker of a boy who sat on my right.

Like most boys who are eager to learn, I was fairly gullible. Carefully tapping the top of my boiled egg with a spoon, before taking the shell away, I felt his hand on my arm. I knew by the glint in his eye that he had planned his 'routine,' and the family knew that he was out for his fun and resigned themselves to, **"Little Jimmy being in for it again."** He beamed, **"There are three ways to open a boiled egg."** I waited, as if for a parachute jump. **"The first is to tap the top with a knife, as I do, then peel away the top. The second is to tap, tap, tap,** with a spoon as you do." He eyed me, as a cat its prey. "And the third?" I asked. **"Like this,"** he volunteered, as he whipped my egg from its cup, then with little ceremony, dropped it on the floor. I retrieved it to a chorus of, **"You zhoulden tease Jimmy like that."** Of course, as soon as we were outside, I attempted to beat him up, though if he took his normal stance, as a massive oak might, I made little impression.

The Flower Show was on its way and the school had lists of things for which children might enter. Living among the wild flowers, I felt little like collecting a large variety of them as an entry. "Wild grasses?" I asked myself, "were there garden ones?" and supposed there were. My family and I in our neck of the woods, spent all our time getting rid of it, so it would have seemed treacherous to collect the vile stuff. "Perhaps woodwork, no, my dovetails were the worst in the school, in spite of training from a master with all the patience of a saint. Cookery was for the girls, as was needlework. Models? No, they fell apart at the merest look, let alone after being transported to the vast marquee in the park. Art then? Oh dear, art." Mine was not of a high standard, as it may be guessed. Not for me those fine black pencil drawings of the stocks, the church and the Manor. Not for me the single flower, which looked more real than those on display when July came.

In utter dismay, amid doom and gloom and when all seemed lost, inspiration came. "Who was to judge the art competition? Why, the Lady of the Manor to be sure. The Lady, the church, art, where had I linked her name with the present problem, where, where? The church, yes the church. Psychology my boy that is what was needed. The church, a window, a window .... The one in memory of her grandparents, that was it! Lots of colour, brilliant colour – brilliant thought! Draw the general shape and bung some colour in. Most important, pay much attention to the lettering. "In Memory of ...." stretching across the bottom. Make the name very black and bold, and continue, "And of Emily his wife." Oh yes, that was it, of course it was, I knew 'it' when I had dreamed it up." Came July, and I watched the villagers viewing my painting – rather its subject, and I watched the judges do the same. Then I waited for the chief judge to hand me first prize. She smiled and I smiled back. I also managed a faint smile for all the clever artists in the school. I was aware of a lesson there, and artists will know it.

Sunday mornings were often bright with sunshine, sparkling dew and the gold-leaf of the fine church decoration. I was glad to be with those I loved and admired for their achievement; best of all, I served at the Altar, and was part of the community that worshipped in that fine building. Sunday afternoon brought the gloom. Dinner was always a large meal, as it was the only day of the week when time could be given to its preparation and consumption. Sleeping at night and in bed was acceptable, but the hateful part of Sunday was the sleeping after dinner, holding, or under a newspaper; that is what parents did and it was very boring. Even more boring than the front page story, **"Hitler Youth ..."** **"They'm a dangerous race,"** my father said. **"Look what they did last time."** He never seemed to mention what we did. I knew he had been wounded in France and had crawled for a mile across No-man's-land, before reaching safety. **"They'm a clever lot at fighten,"** he yawned, speaking of the Germans. I often wondered, if he so disliked the Germans, why at our back door was there a hanging basket, a pickelhaube [spiked helmet] as worn by German officers in the Great War?

Turned upside down and filled with earth, it looked most peaceful with its shamrock and trailing plants. War? I knew little of it, except that in history books it appeared to be romantic. Perhaps it was the comparatively recent war that was boring.

With my parents' descriptions and those of others, I was left in no doubt that the Great War was terrible. Perhaps because of this, they showed no great enthusiasm for the military manoeuvres that took place, with little notice being given to villagers. Farmers may have been given one or two "Out of Bounds" notices, but these made little difference to the skirmish, attack, or retreat of any of the regiments from Southern Command, as tanks, trucks, guns and soldiers battled over cornfields to win a particular 'war.' The War Office would compensate farmers, and the old gate knocked down by a huge lorry was often to someone's advantage.

Those dark nights – or early mornings – were very exciting for a small boy, as our quiet village became a scene of war. It seemed like a dream – to parents a nightmare – that our tiny narrow roads were being used by huge tanks, just like they did in war films, taking over the village, the fields and certainly the minds of the inhabitants. "There's another and another" could be repeated till tired parents had sunk into sleep again, yet still more vehicles came. A mass of implements of war, together with much shouting in strange accents. The officer in his 'Oxford' accent: "Your bloody truck is stuck in the mud." A plaintive reply from a North Country soldier: "Yes Sir, one wheel is stuck." They did not say **stuck** like we did in Dorset.

Summer would come soon, and after a little more dreaming summer came. It brought sections of most of those regiments from Salisbury Plain to the fields around the village. Acres and acres of fascination for a boy to investigate, miles of pipe-lines for water and land-lines for communication and tents by the hundred, to be inspected. The most exciting part of the dream was yet to come true and when it did, I experienced a very special summer of my childhood. Each regiment 'adopted' one small boy as a 'mascot' during the perod of the summer camp, and being chosen by the Royal Artillery gave me 'officer status' for a while, allowing me to come and go within the camp. This included the best seat (the shoulders of one of the men) to watch some of the best variety shows available. ENSA brought to a huge marquee some great artists to entertain the 'cream' of the British Army. I have not owned, all at the same time, so many sweets or bars of chocolate, nor had such a collection of badges, used-rounds of ammunition and pictures of a military nature since that dream-like summer.

Not all was perfect in the village during the summer camp. It could hardly have been expected with hundreds of young soldiers roaming our quiet countryside. All who owned an apple tree were prepared to have it stripped by the end of the summer, and it was left to those with daughters to hope for the best. There was a special code of conduct for those soldiers who came into the village, though it was not always adhered to. Our tiny village hall was taken over by a touring repertory company, who presented a series of plays, to which some of the troops were attracted. As 'mascot' I was present at one of the plays and learned how it felt to be torn between emotions. I was proud to be sitting with a section of 'my' regiment and proud too that I was seeing a professional troupe of actors perform *The Lady Doctor*. On our tiny stage they worked wonders, though the man who sold the tickets at the door was the third party of the triangle, of which the lady, who was the doctor and her husband, were the other two sides. The husband was played in a meek hen-pecked way and the actor wore a ginger wig. Nothing very odd about that, but the performance did not proceed without a hitch.

Young soldiers, after a day of adventure in their chosen life, were not the best audience. Could I have willed them to behave I would have done. Came decision time on stage: "You must choose which one of us ...." The troops joined in the drama. I wished then there was no such word as loyalty. The soldiers rocked with laughter and turned seats over as things got out of control, bringing the play to a halt, and causing the actor in the ginger wig to 'come out of character' to address the audience. "If you cannot behave, then you must leave the hall," he delivered, a little emotionally. They cheered and left, taking their mascot with them. I could not 'desert' Southern Command, though I had deserted the valiant band of actors. Some years later I regretted my decision.

At the end of those happy weeks, in which I received the treatment such as that granted only to royalty, the summer camp drew to a close. Though such tremendous hospitality could not be returned, it was the duty of the 'mascot's' parents to entertain several of the other ranks close to the centre of the social activities of the regiment. It was a Saturday and the house was spick and span. I knew it was Saturday, because the baker had called, as had the butcher, and they only came on the same day when it was a Saturday. The butcher had brought the Sunday joint, and on this occasion, some sausages for Sunday breakfast.

My heroes arrived, looking very smart, and somewhat out of place in an ordinary room. The past weeks in the camp produced quite different men than the shy boys who sat on straight high-backed chairs exchanging formal greetings with my parents, who, and I prayed very hard, would be careful to say all the right things. My father referred to the trenches a little, but perhaps, mellowed by the port – considered the right drink for the occasion – he adopted the line: **"I 'zpect 'tis different now."** My mother spoke of the boys' homes, their girlfriends and their ambitions. During all this I nervously looked around to see that all was in order. I saw our tabby cat for a moment, then assumed she had gone out. She was a 'shark,' the description of a cat that stole from the kitchen table, when one's back was turned. There was a pause in the conversation, when, as if to fill it, the 'something' which I feared, happened. I remind the reader at this stage that my story is factual.

"Oh no," I heard my mother cry, as all eyes riveted on the passageway that led from the larder to the back door. There was our cat, who at that moment I must have hated, as I bit back tears. There was our cat, hauling our sausages away and towards the back door. Had she taken the pile and gone quickly, it would to some extent, have been acceptable to me, but no, holding the first sausage firmly in her mouth, she dragged the whole string – dear God, she dragged them slowly – towards the door. Speechless, for fear of what words might issue from the mouth, everybody sat, as if frozen. I prayed there might be some way of turning the clock back, or pretending the incident never occurred. No, the horror was there and it registered on all those faces, watching, as if they were in an hypnotic trance. "Could it not end quickly?" I thought, "or could someone talk about the weather?" My mother stepped towards the train of sausages, and, as both its and her pace quickened, her foot came down hard on the last carriage, rather sausage.

With the oaths she was shouting at the cat and the sudden jolt, it was forced to let go. Had it all ended there, sadness might have turned to joy, but it did not. My mother picked up the string of sausages, and carefully brushing off each, she refolded them into a neat pile, then took them away, I assumed to the meat-safe. The soldiers said it was time for them to go and soon their lorry sped away, as if in retreat from some unknown force.

The village seemed empty for a time, as we returned to our normal activities. My father to the fields, my mother to her endless washing and scrubbing, and we children to school. The village would not be quite empty, for near the school had camped the Missionaries. No doubt they chose to visit us before the next village in darkest Africa. There they were, camped with their caravan within sight of our church and our church school. What they hoped to achieve there, I had no idea. That we would turn from our wicked ways and repent? As my mother said: **"'Tis like teaken coals t' Newcastle."** There they were, nevertheless, ready to do their missionary work.

Under the old plane trees on the Rec. they set up a portable organ, a lectern and handed out books in which some simple hymns were printed in large lettering. So we gathered to be led into Christian ways. We, who had spent the first hour of our day in church and said other prayers since, gathered, so we might be redeemed. I wonder why we were eager enough to crowd round the organ? Was it because they gave away rather nice 'religious' books, when the singing was over? or because it was fun to sing 'jingly' hymns outside, without the solemn restriction of the church, and with an audience of villagers? True most passers-by remarked: **"What the devil be gwoen on there then?"** An unfortunate choice of words.

"Whiter than the snow, whiter than the snow, ..." we sang. Alas, many of us knew a rather coarse version of that: "Wash me in the water that you washed your dirty daughter," causing some laughter with the group round the organ and so losing any reverent effect that might have been created. I thought then that missionaries, as others, should take in the lay versions of songs or hymns in their education, thereby avoiding a breakdown at the very start. I hoped they would study language and customs before going to those 'heathen lands afar.' They had gone a little astray in their choice of hymn, and the next was not without flaw. The idea was good and the words simple enough to follow through:

"Going astray, going astray, what must I do to be lost? .... "

and continued through the verse on how to get lost. The next verse, to be sung with great joy, went:

"Going astray, going astray, what must I do to be found?
Turn and believe, Christ Jesus receive,
This I must do to be found."

It had a Victorian ring and some poetic licence. I knew that 'receive' was poetic but not right. The word smacked of being used to rhyme with 'believe' and that was not good writing. I hoped those missionaries studied more carefully, before attempting to convert Africa, or they might have headed straight for the cooking-pot.

10

"MAM, MAM, mam, come and look mam, look mam, a airplane," I shouted, with all the excitement of someone discovering the sky for the first time. My mother had plenty of time in which to react, as the plane slowly traversed the area of space above the village. A monoplane might have created greater excitement, but this was only a biplane. With its two wings joined by struts, it was low enough for us to see the pilot and to read its markings. The village looked up, shielding its eyes from the summer sun, as this that, **"Never ought t' be,"** droned across the sky, and eventually merged with the distant blue, looking rather like a clove on the edge of an apple tart, before fading forever. All returned to their labours or their rest, but not without some of the elders saying: **"Ah, we've come t' zummit** [something] **t' be zure we have."**

Everything was slower then, but, fifty years hence, will they not say that of the nineteen eighties? Slowness has always been associated with Dorset, both in speech and action. I do not believe there is truth in the assumption, but even if it was true, it would be the more endearing. Perhaps during the long, seemingly pointless conversations, there was an exchange of ideas, friendship or togetherness that made the village home:

> **"Dost think 'twill rain?"**
> **"Noo."**
> **"Do veel like it."**
> **"Wind be in the wrong pleace."**
> **"Do zometimes rain when 'tis there."**
> **"Not when 'tis blowen hard."**

When all the possibilities and combinations of forecasting had been exhausted, with no conclusion being reached, on their parting one heard:

> **"Zoo, 'ee think it mid** [might] **rain t'mar?"** [tomorrow]
> **"It mid."**
> **"Do veel like it."**
> **"Dost think zoo?"**
> **"I do."**
> **"Have 'ee got yur harvest in?"**
> **"Ah, 'tis all in."**
> **"Dwon't matter then, about the rain?"**
> **"Noo, dwon't matter."**
> **"I dwon't think 'twill."**
> **"It mid."**

So, the meeting ended with nothing great being resolved, but the summer breeze had been complimented with the balm of the Dorset burr.

The description of an event was in the same way often long and drawn-out. A family Christening held a few villages away, producing an enquiry which sounded quite unnecessary. The enquirer knew there were about forty of the family who could have been present, and also knew that only seven attended the ceremony. There were endless questions as to who was present: **"Was George there?" "No." "Or Bessie?" "No."** and so on. It will be seen that the shortest route is in the naming of the seven. A lack of logic? but was there ever logic in the coming or going of the bees in a sunny garden? They buzzed endlessly between hive and bloom, burdened, yet still burrowing for more pollen in flowers far distant, when the hollyhocks near the hive were a rich source of the same pollen. Logic was not applied there, nor was it in the country speech.

"Talk zense," they might have said, but how dull to talk sense all the time. There was no real sense in my Standard 2 story, more a beautiful thought than a story. My teacher explained that some people many hundreds of years before had thought the darkness and the stars at night could be explained quite simply. God, in His wisdom, drew a large curtain across the sun, and as it had many holes, the light shone through, that was the explanation for stars. Though very young, I knew it was nonsense, but that the imagery was beautiful.

In case I have given the impression of a spoil-sport in my approach to school, let me make it clear I was the most difficult student imaginable. It may have been the gipsy, the artist, or for that matter, the animal in me, that made me such a handful. A great deal of my time was spent on the school stretcher with a nose-bleed, caused by a thump over the head, inflicted by a teacher in a last desperate attempt to suppress me. Who rubbed drawing pins under the desk, till the friction made them near red-hot, then pressed them on the back of the neck of the pupil in front? Who pushed a non-swimming child into the pool, then walked proudly away, as the rescuers went to work? and who, by placing a large ball of candle grease on a stove almost burnt the school down? I plead guilty on all counts and ask that all my other crimes be taken into consideration before sentence is passed.

Laughter, helpless laughter. That is one of the greatest gifts of life. Simple things produced it in children and adults. Oddly it was most likely to occur when one was trying to suppress it, as, for example, in church. I assumed that church was so serious that an outlet must be found, laughter was the valve. The word **hassocks** for instance, produced the thought of laughter. Hesitate with the 'h' and the word becomes funny, where as cassocks does not. With such laughter, besides the tears streaming down the face, one needs to take in the sound. The outward blast of sound and the creaking intake of breath, till the next bout.

At Christmas in a Wimborne shop, there was an example of helpless laughter. A good life-size dummy of a man sitting in a chair and holding a glass of whisky. The dummy rocked back and forth, and to the sound of a recording, laughed helplessly. A large notice by it proclaimed: "Just what the doctor ordered," then, "He spotted how low our prices are." The point of my story is that after the shop had closed for the day, and the sound of the record switched off, the dummy continued to rock. I can never forget the expression of the dummy or its movements, especially the backward motion, when the laughter was at its height. Today's equivalent is TV with the sound turned down, which will prove that vision without sound is pointless if the actions are meant to be accompanied by sound.

There was little sound in the village, which made me understand how death can affect a small community. Just behind the barbed wire fence where thunder had appeared to me in the guise of a black sofa, there was a tiny thatched cottage. In it lived, or had lived, a kindly old man with his gentle wife. **"Zhe's gone,"** they said, vowing that the village would never be the same again. I could see no difference, so surely it would not change. Across the field went the woman to do the laying out. She had done a good number in her time and was apt to describe them. I distanced myself from her, lest the details spilled forth. As a child, and now, I like to think of people as in life, and to continue remembering them that way.

The details of the funeral were soon circulating the village. "Abide with me" they sang, and it was very sad. It always seemed to be "Abide with me," but the words fitted the occasion. However, though life was supposed to be short, "Swift to its close ebbs out life's little day," that dear lady was eighty-four, that did not seem terribly swift. Maturity taught me a line from another hymn, "Short as the watch that ends the night," and I knew how swiftly time ebbs out. As soon as the soil had been replaced and the flowers arranged on the mound, there was a rush of villagers to see who they were from. In those days the ink on the written cards ran, so by next day the message may have been "In loving memory, From: Stan" ... or Steve, or Stew? No, there was no Stew in the family. It was best to go before dew or rain made things difficult. I thought then, "People who observe this sadness, do they think, this could be my mother, my father, or, needing much deeper thought, me?" Death? There was too much fun to be got through to think of that. Now overgrown in the old cemetery there is a large tomb, where other boys and I raced to be first to run round seven times, stand still and hear bells. Tradition has it that after the seventh revolution bells can be heard. Did we hear them? I always did, but then I always heard the sea in sea shells. There were strange inscriptions on tombstones, there were glass globes with china flowers and doves, and, above the dead people, were dead flowers. There was the stone that read: "Gone Home to Rest," so off **hwome** we went, rather ran, not to be late for tea.

They often said in the village, especially if one treated a serious subject lightly: **"Zomethen will be zent on y'."** Perhaps I had not been solemn enough during the last three days for what befell me next. The kindly old man, was a lonely old man, now that his wife had gone. **"Jimmy is a good bwoy,"** he told my parents, **"Could 'ee come an' zit wi' me, evenens?"** They had agreed, with the payment of a few shillings a week, that I should do so. Had they known at that time the misery I was to endure, they would not have agreed. There I was, a child of seven, sitting in the dead woman's chair, a child, used to being up and about and in the middle of a happy family environment, transferred to a place of death. There was the wireless with its separate speaker, but silent, and opposite was the old man, dear to me a week ago, but not now, in his grieving. He looked for his partner at each creak of the stairs, while I recoiled in her chair from sheer horror. There were some of her things, a purse, a photograph of them both, when younger, and pictures of older relatives, now dead. There was a picture of him when in the army and a reproduction picture of a battle from the Crimean War – more death. There was an unironed tablecloth, unwashed crockery and there was, to my mind, an air of general decay. "Dear God," I thought, "please deliver me from this."

I could never have been accused of immediate cowardice, though no doubt it crept up on me in the end. There, huddled in his, once favourite chair, was a broken man, lonely and pining for his dead wife. No living person could have filled the emptiness in that house or in his heart, a boy of seven could only make the sadness more acute. I tried to avoid seeing the tears in his eyes, and through sickness at heart, rather than bravery, showed no tears in mine. Bless him now, with his departed, he saw, after a short time, how hateful a task I had been set, and I was, after his consultation with my parents, released. Before that time I had often caught and caged wild birds. I never did so again.

A child must learn, but sometimes things and people are destroyed in the learning. The man who brought the newspapers, always had a broad smile. His smile was a little broader on a Sunday, when my mother, taking the *News of the World* from him, accompanied by a disapproving click of her tongue, might have said: **"Dreadvul in'it, but y' can zee be his picture 'ee's a bad'n."** That was on Sundays. Some weekday mornings he collected bets for horse-races to be run in the afternoon. Very few people who gave him their bets seemed to win anything. Of course he could not help it if the horse lost – that money was lost – but sometimes the horse won and quite handsomely. On these occasions he returned the punter's bet the following day, explaining that he had not arrived back in time to put it on. He used the punters' money for his own gambling and benefit; no wonder he smiled broadly.

There are many beautiful and secluded country lanes in Dorset, and there are some which in my young days were something else entirely. Though they are now overgrown lanes, only identifiable by the little station buildings, they were once proud railway lines. One such line ran between Bournemouth and Salisbury. I said ran, but walked would have been a better description. A journey via this line was often a slow business, which was not the fault of Southern Railway, but that the villages were so close together. No sooner had the engine got up steam, than it came to a halt. Then followed some relaxed talk on the weather and the price of things, while loading took place. Agricultural implements, milk churns and bicycles. Bicycles with their owners and bicycles without, but there were always bicycles. The poor little engine puffed its way uphill, pulling only three carriages, as sleepily as the nestling villages appeared amid the hills, while time passed by. I am constantly referring to the Dorset sense of humour and must do so here. In Scotland in the period of steam trains, they joked: **"Och, while the train's gaen alang, you can get oot an' pick flooers."** Always ready to go one better, we said of ours: **"Vlowers? While the trean be a-gooen along, we can git out, plant 'em, grow 'em an' then pick 'em."**

By train to Salisbury, shopping, tea and then home. Tea was such an important meal. Tea was a social occasion, and **"They'm comen vor tae on Zunday,"** was something very special. Out came the jelly dishes, out came the blancmange dish and out came fruit dishes. All cut glass and precious. Out came the damask tablecloth, out came the silver from their wedding-day canteens and out came the various cake dishes and stands. If memory serves me right, I hated blancmange, and certainly I hated junket. Tinned peaches I loved – better than fresh – but only after all other food had been disposed of and one's taste prepared for the tang, the teeth recoiling from their first impact. The good, almost holy, humour that passed through the conversation was on a par with the meal. If only every day of the week could have been like that.

The evening walk followed, and more pleasant talk. In long languid conversations I became aware of the dialect and how important a part the word **Ah** played. Used instead of "Yes," it had much more variety than that word. It was possible to gather the other person's point of view from the "Ah," of their reply. Depending on the gravity or the humour of what has gone before, the questioner says **"So, you see what I mean?"** The **"Ah,"** in reply may well be anywhere within the range of intonation. The relaxed burr of the dialect matched the breeze wafting over the distant cornfields, which merged into the dark woods beyond. Along the dusty lane and through a gap in the wood, were the dearest things I knew. There, stretching into infinity were my Dorset Downs. No precious carpet was ever kinder to the feet. The Dorset Downs, where Stone Age, Bronze Age, Iron Age and all the ages since have come and gone, yet left something, as each age must. Shall we be remembered, that we, with the plough, destroyed them? When that happened I felt deeply about it and wrote *Harley Down:*

Noo, dwon'ee teake the down away,
　Not thick zof' grass where we did play;
Play all day long – noo, let it be –
　As if it all belonged t' we.
If thee must teake zome, listen, can't
　Thee leave thick bit what zart o' zlant
Down t' the well, ooh do 'ee keep
　A pleace vur wateren o' the zheep.
Vur down thick hill the zhepherd come,
　When his day's wanderen was done,
An' we did walk behin', an' then did run
　Till we jist had t' vall, 'twere vun
T' roll an' roll the rest o' way –
　I 'member jist like yesterday.
If thees must plough, do leave us this,
　An' if thees woussen, leave the pi'ce
Where diddies camped – a precious pleace –
　Wi' zmoke that browned the vaice an' veace,
Brown, like girt big vilbert nuts;
　Not like a barley vield that cuts
The winden paff down t' yon 'ood,
　An' the delights o' childern's vood.
Leave zomewhere vur t' ride a harse,
　Zome blackburries an' zome yaller garse,
An' if thees must destroy all these,
　Vur God's zeake leave they vew vir trees.
If thee dost teake all this away,
　I promise thee there'll come a day,
When Monkton's chapel bell woon't ring,
　Nur will the drush or blackbird zing
Z' loud, nur little vaices zhout;
　Wi' nothen t' be glad about.
They cotton plants, as we did zay,
　I bag thee, leave us zome o' they,
Vur they revlect the purple hue
　O' zunset, jist 'avore it goo
Down; zoo, if vur progress, this must die,
　Thees could, vur all I'm wuth, teake I.

11

I KNEW I must come back to the trim little garden behind the equally neat cottage, at the rear of which was the woodshed. The woodshed had claimed my attention for some time, or rather one corner of it. There, still hanging on a rusty nail, was the coveted alarm clock. It looked so lost out of its environment and I felt I might be helping in giving it a home. No, that is not true. I had seen it over a period of time and desired it, and had studied it from all angles and in all weathers. I had worked out my route, from climbing over the fence, crossing the small garden, then the most difficult and exciting moment, the taking of it from its nail and the quick retreat to and over the fence, to the paradise of a new and exciting possession. At home, there were plenty of bits and pieces of clocks, which I had under repair. I felt in my mind, I would one day be able to start a clock that had stopped – and keep it going. Perhaps I lacked a delicate touch, as I did when catching fish from the river and keeping them in a bath of water, or digging up bulbs to see if they were growing. Did I know my own strength when it came to the 'heart' operation, the hairspring adjustment?

In the past I had only been given parts of old clocks, but here was a complete clock, and surely if wound up, it would go. No, it might need just a *little* adjustment. There lay the root of the matter, for once I began repairing I had no idea when to stop. **"Tidden that that's wrong, so must be this. No, then must be ...."** and so on, till there were many wheels, cogs, screws and connecting pieces strewn on the back shed floor. I knew exactly how and where the bits were fitted back together, but ended up with several spare pieces. I excused myself by saying "It'll go without em," but of course it did not. "See Mam," I said, "When I push this wheel round, it works." **"Then,"** my mother replied sagely, **"I suggest you ztay there pushen the wheel roun', that way you'll be out o' mischief."** Parents were silly, so I went on hooking away at the hairspring until it was a long straight piece of thin wire, instead of a rebounding coil of fine brass.

The house was silent and the garden still. I felt my heart pounding and my mouth dry, as the moment of decision drew nearer. What if I made a noise as I climbed over the wire of the fence? What if I stumbled and fell? What if the back door opened as I entered the garden? Did I just say: "Good afternoon, isn't your garden nice?" Or, horror of horrors, what if the clock was attached to the nail in some way? Having reached my goal I would have no tool to deal with that. What if, what if .... ? No, complete calm, count five, no, go now – and I went!

It is amazing the resources of calm a human being has when the time for action arrives. The rehearsals in my mind had combined too many problems and all the "what ifs?" were thrown aside. Instead of the planned quick dash, I went quietly and quickly over the fence, then walked casually to the shed. Without breathing, as if dismantling an unexploded bomb, I lifted the clock from its nail and put it under my jersey, drawing it to the left side, thus avoiding the bird-nesting hole on the right. A few strides to the fence and over. "There was nothing to it," I thought, but still breathed a sigh of relief. Keeping complete control, I sauntered across the field to the river, where I pretended to be absorbed, yet longed to look at my treasure. I dangled a stick in the water, then along the river's edge to the stile, where I paused to make sure there were no "what have you got under your jersey?" people on the other side. Then a quick dash across the road and through our back door.

The one thing I had not allowed for, then occurred. My mother came from the kitchen just as I was unloading my treasure. The questions began, and my answers followed. I lied, I pretended, I pleaded, but to no avail. I had 'blown it' and knowing my mother's rigidity with rules, I had to admit defeat. "So, that's that," I thought, but that was not that. **"Now,"** said my mother, with a severity I had rarely heard, **"We'm gwoen back wi' that."** "No mam, not me," I complained. **"We'm gwoen back wi' it,"** she repeated. **"We'm gwoen back, and we'm gwoen t' knock at her door, then what are we gwoen t' do?"** **"Dwon't know mam,"** I whined. **"You be gwoen t' hand her that clock, tellen her you've stolen it."** **"No mam, no mam,"** I pleaded, as she took my hand and the clock, setting out for the cottage.

My mother rapped at the door and the smiling lady answered, then looked a little puzzled. Cued, or rather pushed by my mother, I said my piece, while looking anywhere but at her eyes. **"Lard bless 'ee, you can have that wold thing,"** she beamed. **"Oh no he can't,"** said my mother firmly, **"He will not steal from you, nur vrom anybody."** I was dragged off, as the owner of the clock gazed in half amusement and half puzzlement, at a tall stern mother and a deflated little boy being taken home for the trial and sentence which must follow. I knew the Commandments, I knew them backwards; Thou shalt not covet, Thou shalt not steal, and the rest. Words learned parrot-fashion had no effect. Experience that day taught me much.

To my sulking and my comics, most of which had been scanned before. Of the many piles, none were for throwing away, because they could be read for the first time by visitors, or again by me. More important, they were good as swops. My mother called them rubbish, but selecting a book from her shelves, she said: **"This is a lovely book."** Before I mislead you, I must explain that 'lovely' meant it was bound in leather, brown, green or rich-red in colour. The lettering on the cover and spine was tooled in gold. Oh yes, we had some lovely books.

Having admitted some of my wrongdoing, it is safe to say I feel better, but reporting the wrong of others gives an even finer feeling. There were those who put pepper along the edge of one of the church pews. When the verger was missing, they popped in with the pepper and carefully put a line of it along the pew's ledge. When that row was filled with the sweetest ladies kneeling in prayer, all ten of them sneezing more or less together, that was a sight and sound to surprise. The look of "Why should they all catch cold at the same time?" deserved a photograph for posterity.

The same daring boys stole across the wide lawns of the Manor. There, in its huge front porch, shining white in the semi-darkness of the evening, were several marble busts. They set about improving their colouring of pure— white marble and applied liberally to their mouths, deep-red lipstick. Having dealt with each male bust in the same way, they ran for their and their parents' sake. Now that the Lord of the Manor no longer has the power to **"drow me out o' house an hwome,"** I may **nark** on my fellow criminals and tell the world of these things.

I never was satisfied with too calm an existence. If nothing very much happened, then it must be made to. Annoying the Headmaster was one way to create drama. His excellent method of teaching, with the use of models, gave us an immediate idea of the subject. He enjoyed talking on time and space, and often demonstrated space and the movement of the planets by using several oranges, a couple of apples, a cricket ball and anything else that came to hand. Holding them up, as a juggler might, he revolved them all, revolving himself to complete the motion within the demonstration. "There you have it," he would say with conviction, "There it all is, from the nearest planet to the most distant." That was my cue to enquire: "But what is beyond the most distant Sir?" I knew the answer was difficult, but I really wanted to know it; I still do. Perhaps he thought the answer, involving the theory of relativity was too complicated for us, so he put all his planets on top of a low cupboard and departed – to make an important telephone call.

He must have forgiven me, when he saw the praise in my eyes for his latest practical teaching idea; a post office/shop, and it was brilliant. There it stood in the corner of the classroom. Built by senior woodworkers and stocked by those who did hours of handwork, making and painting every item for sale, from butter and sweets to cash and stamps. His plan involved maths and book-keeping, plus costing, ordering and stock-taking. My subject was there too; drama. I was the *most difficult* customer.

That was not his last idea in practical teaching. He was a keen bee-keeper and within the school a company was formed in which each child had a number of sixpenny shares. I am proud to say I was Managing Director of the Company, so that, in all modesty, it must have been well run. The art of bee-keeping, gardening, company accounts, sales of honey and many other things, gave us a good insight on how life might be in the world outside. We were quite professional in our bee-keeping, not at all like a farmer's wife who kept bees, I believe to make her busy life even busier.

On a warm sunny afternoon, she and I saw a swarm of bees in flight. They landed on the branch of an elm tree and soon became a huge swirling mass of workers surrounding the new queen. With great excitement, she hurried to get a skip, which she splashed with sugar water. Upturned, this was placed on the ground below the swarm, ready to accept the queen and most of the bees. She quickly fetched a ladder and a saw and propping the ladder against the branch, she ascended in order to study the position. The object was to lower the branch and the swarm towards the skip, then shake it. Hopefully the queen would drop into the skip, and if she did the bees would certainly follow. At almost the top of the ladder, she began sawing the branch on the *left hand side* of the ladder. Like wiping up a washed plate, when one knows it is about to fall, I stood transfixed. I wanted to warn her, but a stronger desire was to see the branch, the bees, the ladder and her sink slowly to the ground. Mild sadism? Found, I suspect in many children.

That was a sunny day. There was a day soon after which began sunny, but the thoughts of us all must have brought the clouds. "End of the World" the newspapers announced. This was a time when most of us thought a little more about religion and many 'crackpot' societies were formed. The end of the world was a favourite subject, it ended every few months. It was almost as common as stopping smoking – again. However, this announcement was taken more seriously, and many of the newspapers carried the news days before and on 'the day.' Even those who laughed it off took some precautions. I left home for school with my sister Iris, firmly convinced that I would not see home or family again.

The time for the end was at two thirty that afternoon. The clouds gathered at about two and the school felt as if it, and everything beyond its walls was doomed. Staff nor pupils could concentrate and the atmosphere was intense by half past two. The church clock struck the half hour and we waited and we waited and waited – and waited. I am able to tell you my story, which is proof that we waited in vain. Many people said: **"Dwon't vurgit, we'm in the Zilly Thirties,"** and this was an example of what they meant.

The sun was shining by the end of the school day and the walk home along the dusty road was hot and tiring. Our bungalow, near the river, was simple, yet a cool and pleasant place, in which to remove dusty sandals half full of grit from a two mile walk. The front door, though opened, was not used during the summer. It had a large step which was pure-white from several recent chalkings. Spilling over each side of the step were large clumps of pink shamrock, the flowers wide open in the hot sun. Inside, on a polished table, stood a large vase of sweet peas set among asparagus fern, which gently swayed in the breeze from the front door.

At the end of the garden where the taller flowers grew, summer daisies also swayed in the breeze. There, an unfamiliar clump of mixed flowers moved up and down, then spoke: **"Ah, you be hwome."** My mother, in her floral overall, bending over the flower bed and taking out yet another piece of couch grass, had spotted me. A long cool drink of water from the well bucket, then the throwing off of clothes and the thought of school. My mother came in from the garden and called: **"Cheange yer zhoes as well min'."** She busied herself with the business of cooking tea. Later, in the cool of the evening, she would return to the garden, stand close to her night-scented stock and say yet again: **"I be vond o' they."**

Cooked tea was of the simplest food, but simple food can be very enjoyable. It was common to hear my parents say: **"You childern have never gone hungry."** That was true, I feel sure they would have eaten less to enable us to have more. After a good filling meal, my father might be heard to comment: **"The King coulden do better. The King can wonly 'ave a bellyvul."** My mother had her own view of the royals, rather 'picture book,' but loyal. **"Well, they do have zoo many little bits an' peaces. They dwon't eat like we do, but they can pick an' choose. All off gwold pleates too** [common enough view] **a different pleate vur everythin'. Waited on hand an' voot, they be. Jist git out o' bed an' zomebody d' dress 'em an' git their breakvast an' wash up atter 'em."** She might pause for thought, then add a little more to the already familiar fiction: **"Course, they dwon't never wear nothen twice. Put it on they do, t' wopen zummit or 'nother, then it be took back t' the zhop. Course 'tis good advertisement vur the zhop. Dwon't never zee 'em in nothen twice do 'ee?"** Well, in distant Dorset we did not see them often enough to check and record the contents of their wardrobes. In these days of exposure to all aspects of the media and the knowledge that royalty wear things much as the commoner does, it is difficult to understand the limit of publicity, even just fifty years ago. I was often left wondering if those stories were repeated in a fable-like way, because my mother knew quite well that the gentry bought good things, but bought them to last. I quote her: **"Tis the poor that keeps the traders gwoen."**

"They'm gwoen at Michaelmas," sighed my father. Said on the 22nd of

60

September, it meant "they" would be leaving in a week, on the 29th. **"Gwoen to a varm ner Zherburne,"** [Sherborne] he continued. One week's notice and the people who were friends, part and parcel of the village, were gone. Children who had been in our team for play were gone, gone forever. The other side of the county was a long way to go in the nineteen thirties. The grapevine might reveal something years from then: **"Zid** [seen] **anything of 'em, zince they went?"** or **"Be they ztill down Zherburne way?"** and the tragic end of the questions: **"The eldest bwoy will be growed up be now I z'pect."** Yes, autumn was a sad time for so many reasons, but chiefly because summer was at an end. It might have been a mistake to turn to the gramophone for solace, for the record then so popular, had a lyric which ran: "The leaves so brown came tumbling down, remember, that September, in the rain."

Autumn was limbo time. When winter came, it brought Christmas and that was bound to be exciting. "What shall we have this year mam, shall we have ... ?" and so on. The normal reply was: **"We must wait an' zee."** However, this lead-up to Christmas was strange. There were whisperings, not exciting ones like, **"I've put it away,"** and **"I've paid some on it,"** no, there was a lot of doubt. I overheard odd things like: **"Well, if 'tis early, I'll be up an' about, but if 'tis vull time, well then ... sp, sp, ..."** All this to me was nonsense. Christmas could not be early or late – though it so often seemed to lag – it was on December 25th and that was that. **"Zhe'll look atter me, an' the childern, an' git the nuss** [nurse] **an' that."** I was eventually told I was to have another little sister for Christmas. **"Don't wanna a sister, mam, I want that train- set, that goes round a figure of eight track, not just round in a circle. I'd rather have a train-set."** The usual reply, **"We shall see,"** from my mother, making just a little bit of a face, as if she had eaten sour apples. Too late in the year for apples, perhaps it was growing pains, that is what they told me. **"You've got growing pains, mam,"** I ventured. **"Perfectly right,"** she said, smiling and causing my father to laugh. I really could not see how my diagnosis could be regarded as a laughing matter!

The odd preparations continued, with a considerable number of 'ifs' scattered among what should have been certainties. Christmas morning always came when it was dark – that is for children – but this year it did so for my parents. A good deal of commotion from the lady next door, who was giving orders: **"Git the nuss,"** [nurse] and my father going off to get her. She arrived as the bells rang on the Christmas morning of 1932 and it was some time before I understood her first remark: **"That's a nice Christmas present."** It was my sister **Darthy** [Dorothy]. There was considerable joy for the adults, but little for the children. We had lost sight of our mother and gained a sister, who we could not yet see. What is more, being told by an outsider, no matter how kind, to **"Goo on out t' play,"** was not my idea of Christmas.

12

"DWON'T YOU dare touch," my mother commanded. She, by raising one finger and my father without raising one at all, made it known to us children how the law stood, and to advance beyond the legal line would invite a smack. Once established, our parents' look was often enough to deter the would-be vandal. In our home there were many areas to be avoided. Beautiful things lead to fascination, and the need to handle, both young and old feel that need. There were shelves of fine china which were well out of reach, and could be pointed at by an adult, who might explain. The whatnot was packed with treasures, some of great value, others merely sentimental keepsakes. Little pairs of china chickens, boots, shoes and numerous figures. A china gramophone, a watch and a number of dishes, which were presents from this resort or that. So they stayed, those little treasures, except at dusting or spring cleaning time.

The dresser took up the length of one wall and on it were the main sets of china, but not that in daily use. Two Victorian oil lamps at the base, then each shelf rose with lines of plates, in front of which were saucers and on the many hooks, cups of every description. At the very top were two glass cases, in which were stuffed squirrels. They looked so out of place in cases gathering dust. The squirrels in the woods looked much nicer. There were two things of great interest on the dresser. One was a Chinese man with a nodding head. The problem was its head needed to be started off and as it was covered by a large glass dome, its removal was no job for a child. "Mam, come and nod the man," nothing. "Mam, come and make the head nod." "Later," she replied. "No mam, now," I pleaded. "I'll nod your head if you dwon't ztop pesteren," she would eventually say.

"Well then mam, can I have a spin?" A spin must be explained. A biscuit tin that once contained biscuits, emptied soon as a result of: "Can I have another one please?" The box was empty, but the best part was left. The lid had a knob at the centre of the top. Nothing unusual about that, but, this knob was capable of spinning and when it did, it took a disc round with it. Marked on the disc were fortune predictions; "Money is coming your way," "A dark stranger is about to propose" [what, I wondered?], "Success is yours," and the like. As none of these were the ones I had spun for, another spin was essential, and another – and another and – Slap! "Now goo on out t' play an' dwon't zhow yur veace till dinner time."

I went to play, and hurried out to avoid taking my sister Iris with me. What boy wanted girls around when he was playing in the river bed? On my exit, as the bungalow was the nearest dwelling to the road, I was asked directions to a certain house two villages away. I knew this to be a professional job, so I called my mother. "Now let me think," she began. Then followed directions on these lines: "Mrs. Dailey, 'zept her name idden Dailey now, 'tis em, now what is her name? 'Tis Webb, noo West, least I think 'tis West. Noo, I dwon't think 'tis. Well now, never mind, her name used t' be Dailey. Now, avore zhe remarried, zhe lived at – do you know I can't remember where zhe used t' live. Her mother used t' live there too. Now zhe d' live near Blandvurd – her mother I mean." By this time the man had taken out his pocket watch and was making distinct signs. If I could give my mam's shoe a slight tap she might have got the message. More often she did not, but grumbled:

"**Ztop doen that,**" so I tugged her apron strings, and she echoed: "**Will you stop it.**" Ah well, I had tried.

"**Now 'tis jist this zide o' Vordin'bridge** [Fordingbridge]**, zhe d' live. Now, imagine you be turned t'other way, you goo ztraight down the road and turn on yur left hand,** [those were her words] **turn on yur left hand be Mrs. Gould's, tha's the hwouse wi' the red curtains, I dwon't like red, d' you? z' common. Then goo on vur 'bout a mile an' you come to a zignpwost. 'Tis a 'ooden 'oone, an' you can wonly read 'oone name on it, tha's Ver'ood.** [Verwood]. **Well, dwon't teake thick 'oone, 'cos that idden the way. Teake the 'oone tha's pwointen t' the right an' goo on up the leane t' Croney's Varm – well, now 'tis White's, but yers avore my time 'twas Croney's. Now, where you zee a lot-a mud in the road, tha's jist a leane, zoo goo on past that, an' you'll zee a road tha's got a zign, Lower Bissett. Well now, I can't 'member what way you d' turn there, but if you back back a bit –**" I have to intercept, "Mam, the baker's here." "**Tell'n t' wait. Ah, back back a bit t' the varm, an' ask vur Rosie, tha's Rosie Durnford, as used t' be. 'Member me to her and ask her when I can have me wateren- can back, an' zhe'll tell 'ee where the Dailey's d' live. Mind 'ee, I yerd as how they'd moved, but I dwon't knoow whether 'tis true.**"

By this time the enquirer was mentally lost, with the thought of being lost in every other sense. Winding up with the starting handle, his bull-nosed Morris, he climbed aboard, only to find the road too narrow to get past the baker's van, who now ensconced with a cup of tea, was checking through the list of deliveries. "**We didden have no gammon, zo I brought 'ee zome ztreaky, will that do?**" To which my mother grudgingly replied "**Have to, I z'pose.**" Then there was the ordering, as my mother glanced out of the window, saying: "**Wha's 'ee messen about vur?**" as she eyed the driver attempting to get through a space only half the car's width. "Mam," I tried. "**Be quiet will you,**" she said. The baker, having lit a cigarette, was prepared for gossip and my mother only too ready to produce it: "**Not another, 'tis less than a ye'r zince t'other. Is it his, do 'ee think? well I never ...** " A roar from the car outside as it reversed a quarter of a mile to make a detour.

I prayed for Christmas to come soon and it came very slowly. I sometimes wondered if God misheard me. Did He, with all the other problems, think I asked that it go quickly? No sooner were the stockings filled, than they were as empty as pockets and the cold and callous days of January. Then was the time to pray for the summer outing to come very quickly. One July day by the sea was as close to Heaven as many country people dared aspire. It was to be Bournemouth that year. "**Dwon't like it,**" my parents chimed, "**Too posh. Tea at the Pavilion, bah, 'tis all chocolate ceakes an' orchester.**" A section of the Municipal Orchestra played there. Still Bournemouth it was to be. There was no doubt that the beach was one of the best along the South Coast – the bits one could see between the bodies, which, like frying sausages, had to be turned now and again.

The great day arrived and we were all up early, waiting an hour before the charabancs arrived. A red one and a yellow one with hoods let down, waited for us to trample over the wet and dewy bank of grass, to settle in our seats. Settle, after some argument as follows: "Mam, can I drive the bus?" and "Why can't the driver sit with us?" Having finally squeezed into the back seat, off we went, with the occasional squeal of delight as we bounced over hump–backed bridges. **"Can 'ee zee the zea?"** my father eventually called to us. Suddenly we saw it, and the world became a magic place. Sand as far as the eye could see, and sea that stretched into the heat-haze until it joined the sky.

Even on the beach it could not be a complete holiday. One, so often me, must watch out for the deck–chair attendant. Parents relaxed in deck- chairs till the warning came, then they slid to the sand till he passed by. Ice-cream – real ice-cream – was on sale under the pier. Rich deep-yellow, made with real cream. Its only fault, that of melting in the mouth too quickly. My mother remarked: **"Like ztrawburries, 'oone d' meake 'ee want vur mwore."** Punch and Judy were there too. Much too vicious was Punch, even in fun. "Judy, Judy, Judy, bang, bang, bang. Bring up the baby Judy, bang, bang, bang." Not very good theatre, I thought – but of course I watched.

Near the pier was a man making pictures. On this occasion he produced a fine one of Mary and Joseph with the donkey. The method was that of the sun shining through grains of sand on to a plate [xerox] which gave a dotted picture similar to those seen in newspapers, and onlookers gasped as the picture appeared.

There was a great deal of digging to be done and much building of sandcastles. **"Mam, I want t' go,"** I moaned. **"What, number one?"** my mother yawned. **"Ye',"** I said, cross-legged. **"Down in the hole, goo on, noobody'll zee y',"** and nobody did. There was the Skylark. My mother, disgusted by the suggestiveness of the word, said **"You'll never git I on 'oone 'o they."** I admired those who, roaring with laughter, went on, and for, the skylark.

If the heat on the beach became too intense, there were the shops to be visited. Many fine and very expensive shops which aimed at the upper class, could not hold our interest. The best store for us in those days was **Woolworse** [Woolworths] where everything was threepence or sixpence. Many mementos and sticks of rock had to be purchased, and it was a case of remembering who had said, before we left: **"Bring us a ztick o' rock min'."** I wondered why parents always stopped to look at the most uninteresting things. Being dragged by the arm, just as one's interest was at its most keen was a little off-putting. **"We'm gwoen t' British Hwome Ztores now,"** was the explanation.

That was the day, and that was the store, in which I nearly broke my heart – for the first time. There we were, scanning the delights of the store, a store displaying so much within reach of our pockets, when there was a wild cry from my mother.. A cry? more a scream than a cry. The rest of the family froze, thinking she had been attacked by some sea monster – but not the lifeguard – as half of the customers and some of the staff looked in the direction of her cry: **"I've lost ten zhillen."** Ten shillings, half a pound, was a lot of money then and half in fact of our shopping money for the summer outing. **"Tis all I got,"** she repeated. **"I had it when I come in, an' now 'tis gone."** "Dear God," I thought, "if only I, if only someone could have given her just that amount, so she could smile again, but praying would do no good here."

"Awfully sorry you have lost some money," said the Manager, "Of course if we find it, we will keep it for you." My mother, in tears, needed none of his reassurance: **"That'll never be vound,"** she said, stifling her sobs, as Rose, a good friend, stuffed a ten shilling note into her bag. Then began the long argument with most of Bournemouth watching the performance. **"Noo, I** coulden teake it, you'll need it yerzelf. Noo 'twas my vault an' I must goo wi'out." and so on. Mothers! My only way out was to pretend Rose was my mam.

Rose and her sister Lil were middle-aged to elderly. Both very sweet and I was fond of them. Rose was tall and spindly with an unwell look, and her expression was that of a mountain goat in a poor grass season. Lil was the opposite, short, tubby and an overall odd shape. The tragedy of the lost money was soon left behind, as we entered the amusement park. Here was a place in which to spend a few more pennies. Little roundabouts, swings and games that offered good prizes. There were the huge glass domes, containing valuable items. A crane descended after the insertion of a penny and scooped up things. In went my penny and, breathless, I waited for a gold watch to be picked up. It grabbed the watch, together with a number of small sweets which formed a bed for the precious things. Then, dropping the watch, it spewed a few sweets down the chute into my hands. Time and time again I fed it my money. When I gave up, a scruffy local boy tried his penny and received a good present. "Rotten machine," I thought, but that Bournemouth boy must have had some knowledge of it.

"Rose, come on, let's go an' look in the looken-glasses," my mother called from the far end of the arcade. The **looken-glasses** were the distorting mirrors. This was my mother at her most jovial – and unkind! Rose and Lil were already distorted by nature and she really wanted to see some further distortion. "Come on, look at me," she persisted, "What a zketch I be, did 'ee ever zee anything z'vunny? What she really meant was, we shall see something very much funnier. My mother at thirty five was, as they said: "A zmart peäce." [piece] Smart, in that she held herself well, had a good figure and walked well.

Soon my mother would be doubled up with laughter, pointing at a vision, or two visions in the mirrors. Unable to speak, she would point, then gasp between each fit of laughter, sounding near to choking as the rebound of sound came from her tyhroat, when it became essential to breathe again. Even as a boy I had doubts about a farcical situation, and this one was doubtful. I had the feeling that for laughter to be fair at another's expense, all should start off with the same advantage, so that the situation developed from that. I hoped as Rose and Lil looked into those distorting mirrors, that as nature had been a little unkind, the mirrors would be kinder and 'de-distort' them into beauties. The mirrors were extremely unkind. Even I, feeling for them and laughing with them, laughed at them, guiltily, but heartily.

The time came for the emptying of sand from buckets, shoes and the turn-ups of dad's trousers. How I was to carry a bucketful of sea home to the village, I did not know, so it had to be left on the beach. The bucket would be a constant reminder of a glorious day. We felt sadness in the journey home through the reddish-purple of the sun over the Dorset hills, as the charabancs took us further from the golden dream of the day. Sad too, was the singing of the adults, though it was meant to be wearily happy. Alas, parents generally sang songs of the past, and in those days the songs of the past were sentimental ballads. *Home Sweet Home* was not a tactful choice, when that is where our little feet would toddle for the next three hundred and sixty four days. Somewhere towards the end of the dismal concert would be, *Show me the way to go Home,* an even worse choice. True, I might have said, "I'm tired and I want to go to bed," but that was nothing to sing about! I do not remember arriving home, I only remember the next morning and that it was not the day of our summer outing.

Old songs, old things and old haunts, childhood memory is often made up of such things. I hated being told to do things, but those I devised myself, no matter how odd, I did with great enthusiasm. One of those things was our picnic. An old gramophone with even older records, mounted on an equally old pram, did not present, in the speech of today, a "With-it" image. These were the 'basics' we children took on our picnics.

A mound of food, which included sandwiches, biscuits, a variety of cake, a flask of tea and several bottles of lemonade, were packed into the bottom of the pram. A couple of cushions, a car rug and various books were added to the iron rations for the hazardous trip. We were bound for Harley Down, almost visible from our starting point. Less than half a mile brought us, panting, to our favourite spot on the downs; that is, had the gipsies not camped there first. We must have looked, not unlike them, as we traipsed with all our worldly goods, so it seemed, to pitch camp. The sun clouded and we wished we had bat and ball for rounders.

Picnicking was a serious business, it needed organising and I was the one to do that. Determined that we should enjoy ourselves, I failed to realise that enjoyment in this way cannot be determined. The weather, the mood of other children, the close proximity of the gipsies, who, after all, were professionals, made me aware that dreams, like those of thatched cottages with roses round the door, so often do not work out. Perhaps it was unforgivable for a country boy not to have guessed these things. I had seen the thatch removed and replaced on the cottage roof, seen a garden ruined – and the roses – by the rotting straw, some twenty years old, as it was thrown over the lovely flowers. I had seen too, the face of a cottager, when the 'dung' was spread over a treasured garden and heard the remark: **"Gi' I a modern house anytime."**

No, I should have seen that some picnics, like some dream cottages, were not as imagined. The trek home was accompanied by dismal 'look-backs' at other picnics. Arriving home less than an hour after setting out was no surprise to my mother, as she remarked: **"I z'pect you've come hwome vur tae."** Humiliating thought, but nevertheless, true. I made excuses, saying: **"Louise and Stan coulden come, so we had to come home,"** and added a little moan, **"And they promised." "Ah,"** said my mother, **"Jist you remember, promises an' pie crusts be meade t' be brwoken."**

"What is for tea, mam?" I said. **"Bread and butter,"** I was told. "Boring," I thought. **"Watercress,"** she added. That was better; in a large glass bowl, one picked it out as needed. "And?" I shouted. **"Jam zan'wich,"** she replied, scraping out the last of the raspberry jam from a two pound pot, no, not the last, a little was left. "Can I clean it out, mam?" I cried. **"No you can't,"** she scolded, taking the jar outside and filling it with water. **"It's vur the wopsies,"** [wasps] she called back. There sat the jam pots, near the back door, for the wasps to visit and drown in their search for jam. The theory was good, but the practice bad. The wasps were enticed to the pots, where they queued up, the overflow entering the kitchen, anxious to take the jam from my piece of sandwich. I left my mother to do the chasing to the window and the murdering. **"Tha's another that woon't zting noobody,"** she said, viciously, but my mind and mouth were too engrossed to say: "Yes mam."

13

THE TERM began with my movng up to the next class, which meant the end of
fooling, as the business of learning became more serious. This class was next door
to the Remove and that is somewhere I had no wish to be, though how I avoided
it, God alone – with all respect – knows. Remove, Remove, it had an awful ring
to it and was not funny at all, as some of my comics suggested: "Bunter of the
Remove." No, the Remove was sinister, and children who were not quite – you
know – went there; not quite bright, they meant. Well I may have been lazy, but
I was bright enough – when it suited my purpose – and I had no intention of
dropping enough marks to be removed to the Remove. So I concentrated a little
more, at least till story time, then my mind departed to wherever the story was
set.

The new girl of twenty, who was our teacher, should not have been a teacher at
all. She should have been an actress, for in her reading she played all the parts as if
they were real, till at the end of chapter six it was time to go home, that was, after
the chorus of: "Oh Miss, just another bit." The journey home on a dull afternoon
with the mundane conversation of inane children, seemed incredibly dull after her
reading. As a teacher we described her as 'OK,' but as a story-teller she was
superb. My mother said of sweet peas, **"The zcent do drug I."** Her reading
voice did that to me. I waited for her at the end of class so that I could carry her pile
of books home, not because I wished to carry the rotten old books, but because I
wanted to be engulfed with the charm of her voice: "Jimmy, will you carry my
books for me?" Would I? I would have carried ten times that for her, still bearing
the brunt of the others' remarks, "Jimmy is a teacher's pet."

I dallied even more than usual on my return home. The bungalow was no place
to be during its redecoration, there was chaos during the operation, and it often
looked worse after the 'stampede'. My father knew people in the decorating trade,
in fact he did a great deal of furniture restoration himself. Being in the know, he
never purchased paint, he merely had the odd tins that were surplus to stock, or
bad colours that no right-minded person would buy. First came the ceilings with
two coats of whitewash. Whitewash was lime mixed with water and applying it
to a ceiling was an art in itself. It needed constant stirring, or the result was a
ceiling washed with water, as lime bespattered the floor. The woodwork was
given coats of brown, beige, or deep-cream paint; paint with a very high gloss,
which took about a week to dry. As we had to live in, and move around the rooms
all that time, we bumped, pressed, placed hands on, or rubbed clothes on each
surface, and the high gloss soon became matt, matt with the most interesting
patterns of coat material, thumb prints, and marks which were not even human.
Who could have expected our tabby cat to step over a window-sill which had been
her walking place night in, night out?

My mother might have worried my father for two or three years before the
redecoration was done, having given up pleading for the vegetable garden to be
dug. **"There,"** he said, when it was completed, **"How's that?"** and waiting with
the smile of a boy. **"Not bevore time,"** answered my mother, **"Now ...."** but
he had gone, though not opening time, gone with his pals for a little relaxation,
apart from throwing the occasional dart. Some of the much-married men in the
bar said: **"I woulden dare walk out, when me wife be given orders."**

"**Nothen to it,**" said my father, "**'Tis the gwoen back that worries me.**"

Like him, I dared things, a characteristic I am proud of. There I was, quite a small boy, two storeys up in the hayloft, standing with the trap doors open and looking forty feet below at the cobble-stones. "**We dare y',**" the boys said. "**How much?**" I questioned. There was consultation. "**Zixpence,**" the leader volunteered. "**O.K.,**" was my brave answer. Standing there, I knew everything was at stake, and if I backed out now I would be reckoned a coward. There was nothing for it, even if death was instantaneous. I knew how the parachutist felt, I knew more, for he had something to hold him in the air and I ..... "Fool," I thought – in mid air. The others only wished to see a little drama: "Sorry Mrs. Attwell, but your son Jimmy is dead." I could not allow that sort of wallowing in emotional claptrap. I landed on my feet and the whole world seemed to throw its weight up at me. My knees came up and crashed into my chin, as I saw all the signs from stars to rays of shock, that I had seen as I pored over my comics, showing the impact of a solid force against an immovable object. They gathered around me as vultures at the kill. Perhaps it was that which made me rise from the ground, wipe my hands, collect my sixpence and walk round the corner of the farmyard wall into our garden, before the tears of pain came. They lasted a short time, because I knew I had won a battle and my praise would be sung in school and the surrounding villages as the boy who had "jumped a hundred feet to his death, but because of a miracle, he lives."

Not much could be said about my heroism at the farm, as we were strictly out of bounds in the hayloft. We were more strictly offside in the hayrick at the top of the lane. You will observe I said, 'in.' It took four boys and I much time to turn a hayrick into a house, but it was done. We scooped out, handful by handful, a vast amount of hay, until we had made a passageway. Then we added one or two rooms, even propping some holes in the side of the rick with spars, to make windows. I shudder today, when I think of the weight of hay above us as we played in our house. All those hours, days, weeks, spent in proximity to certain death, yet, they were exciting times.

In the winter that followed, and only a few yards from our hayrick house, a foul deed occurred. A deed that remained a mystery. In the woods surrounding the estate was much game, and late in the night the beams of torches could be seen as poachers sought out the roosting pheasants. Though the poachers worked silently, they carried shot-guns and would certainly have used them in a tight corner. As a result, the local bobby kept well away when a couple of van-loads of poachers were 'out for the kill.' Among the gamekeepers that night, one was brave, or so it was thought. When he failed to return in the morning, the alarm was raised and he was found; found in a bad way, wounded and in odd circumstances. Police and detectives questioned all for the slightest lead. My mother said: "**I hope they dwon't think 'twere I that did it.**" When the keeper died the enquiry became much more serious.

Where and who were the poachers who came and went in the night, the night not a soul heard the vans or saw torch beams? If there were no poachers, was it an accident? His own gun fired, the spent cartridges proved that. Did he trip, or did he spot a poacher and fire at him? The oddest theory was that the gamekeeper, known to be unhappy, 'set up' the accident. He trigged his loaded gun in the fork of a tree, and attached a slender branch some distance away, so that it would

68

'trigger' the gun. The whole thing to appear natural – if that is the right word. "Was the gun found a distance from him?" they asked. "No," the Sherlock Holmes replied, "It was by him, but he was quite capable of crawling to it after the shot." Such sinister goings-on in our serene beechwoods was the sort of nightmare we hoped would soon pass. It passed, but produced no real answers to some difficult questions.

Another double-barrelled gun fired, but on a Saturday afternoon, and that was all in fun. It fired as the car arrived to collect a wedding couple. **"Bwoth o' them travelen together,"** warned my mother, **"Tha's jist asken vur bad luck."** **"Why mam?,"** we asked. **"Well, the bride must never zee the bridegroom avore they be at the altar, 'tis the wuss** [worse] **luck out."** She spoke as if she was at least privy to the rules between Heaven and the Anglican Church, as they affected ordinary people. These two, however, were not ordinary, for both were gipsies, though living in a farmer's cottage. All had joked about them getting married in the normal way and in our rather grand church. **"Zurprised us,"** they said, **"When the banns were called."**

The car climbed the short hill to the gap, across which, barbed wire stretched to keep the cows in. The wire removed, I watched the black shiny car enter the field in much the same way that the black sofa had on that thundery day. It went slowly across the field to the house of the bride and groom. The man with the gun, who was ready for the salute, looked worried. **"Tis gone half past two now,"** he commented. **"Wedden were vur half past."** At last they appeared, the gun was fired and everybody cheered. They arrived at the church at three, and were turned away, so they made other plans – to live together, not in the cottage, but in the shelter of caravan and canvas.

Except for particular subjects, school was not the place, above all others, where I wished to be. Excuses had to be found and they were very varied. My mother dreamed up things for me to do – **"Childern zhould learn what work do be."** – so she presented the reasons for absence:

"Jimmy has a cold
  Jimmy has a belly-ache [they were not 'polite' notes]
  Jimmy has a hole in his shoe – and it's raining
  Jimmy has [having run out of reasons] to look after me."

If non-attendance was over a long period, or at regular intervals for short periods, the attendance officer was likely to call. The task in which one was engaged might have hurriedly to be left, in order to look suitably indisposed when he called. He very rarely believed any of the excuses, but in my judgement of him, he would have needed to check for a sign of breath with a mirror, then close the eyelids before whistling between his teeth and saying: **"Quite, quite, he couldn't go to school like that."** On second thoughts, if suitable transport could have been found, he might have shipped the child to its class-room, on the grounds: **"Better it should not die ignorant."**

The visiting school nurse was a little more kindly, but still severe. **"Looken vur vermin,"** they said. "Are frogs vermin?" I thought, as she put two flat sticks into my mouth. "People talked of having a frog in the throat. Vermin though, were surely rats and things?" One very scruffy boy had vermin. **"Where?"** I asked, **"In his head,"** they replied. "Dreadful," I thought, "to have rats in his hair." Gradually vermin explained themselves and I came to know that even the best children had vermin, especially the girls with very long hair. There was a great deal of irony in the response to the discovery of nits in a child's hair. The dirty child's parents merely said: **"So what?"** while the parents of the unfortunate children who had been infected, found the disgrace almost too much to bear. I believe the parents of the children who escaped the misfortune were to blame. They said nothing of the dirty child or its parents, but of the clean child, now infected: **"She's got nits, you know,"** without the least bit of sorrow being shown.

"You're a nit, what are you?" my new teacher announced, and I replied, **"A nit Sir."** 'Sir' seemed odd as a title, as it had been 'Miss' up to now. He was strange, but kind, and being young, taught with great aggression. When things were put on the black-board, they were put there for a reason – "Wake up you" – that was me. He had the most vicious and accurate aim with stubs of chalk that my tingling face had ever known. I do wish he had practised his shooting on others a little.

I was glad when my sister Darthy was big enough to be led by Iris and then by me to audition for parts in my show. They were not very good at that age, but as they were the only applicants, and as my mother said: **"Baggers can't be choosers,"** they were given the parts. The trouble was, they were both girls and did not understand the technical side of the theatre, for that matter, that side of anything. My theatre in the daytime, was my bedroom at night, or rather, one end of it was the theatre. The exit from stage right was into a passage, which acted as the dressing room. Oddly, as soon as the curtain went up my mother began cleaning the passage. I believe it was something to do with ownership; possession is nine points of the law and all that. Only gipsies, in her opinion, went on the stage – and how I longed to be a gipsy. My mother's enunciation of the word 'actress' was as if she herself had been to RADA. Oh yes, her 'actress' was the lowest form possible. Even a model was better than an actress. He married a seamstress, he married a waitress, but "He married an – *actress!*" No woman could have been more scathing of her gender.

The curtains for the stage were made of crepe paper – we had no fire officer – and they had to be worked by me, as my sisters had little patience with things like that; **"Let's go an' play hop-scotch."** Indeed, the rise of the curtain showed they never could learn their parts, which I had so carefully written. True I had created the leading role for myself and what was left was minimal. Darthy and Iris agreed there was only one way to say "Yes or no." They were far from right, but I got their drift.

Having got the curtains apart, one, automatically and the other by brute force, I took up my position, having shouted to my mother to be an audience. Yes, she would be and she was – entering half way through the drama and reaching the auditorium via and amid the most dramatic scene. I began again: "Then you must die, you must die, unless you tell me where the treasure is." To which Iris, in a good stage whisper replied (understudying for Darthy): "She's gone to the lav, so I'll do it for her: No, no, no." To which I said: "It isn't fair mam, is it?" and, with great sympathy she replied: **"Things of nature have to be attended to."** So we began again, and my mother cut in, **"I can't ztop long, I gotta ceake in the ob'm"** [oven].

70

Press on, was the only hope. Darthy arrived back from her hurried visit, and was lost within the play, so I hissed: "You go off stage left." To which she replied: **"Tha's inta the cupboard, I'm not gwoen in there, not with the tiddies** [potatoes] **an' apples an' maybe rats."** In all of theatrical history, this must be the point where actor-managers retire. I did, but only till the next production, which would be delayed, as my mother wanted to clean out the cupboards. Clean them out, in order to store the new potatoes, the new apples and no doubt, in due course, the new cork-popping wine.

"Perhaps I could find drama in some other corner of life," I thought. There seemed to be drama in my mother's approach to the visiting tradesmen, but in studying it, I found it akin to farce. **"I beant gwoen t' have any mwore o' that tough beef,"** was shouted at the butcher. He and his ancestors had been 'the butcher' to us and our ancestors, and both sides knew it would continue. "I'll bring a good piece next time," he promised. **"You'd better,"** shouted mam, then coming in, **"Tha's told'n."** She knew, as we all knew, he had not been 'told' at all.

"Dwon't you ever bring I ztale bread agean," to the baker, **"I needed t' cut it, or you'd have had it back,"** she continued. The baker had been a friend of the family for years. He gossiped with gran and my mother, bringing all the news and scandal with him. Suffering the odd stale loaf was a small price to pay for that.

"I dwon't want big lumps, nur do I want it too zmall. I jist woon't have a lot o' zlack an' dust," my mother instructed the coalman. He grinned through the grime on his face; at least I assumed it was a grin, it could have been a snarl through all that coal dust. **"I z'pose it have bin out in the wet t' meake it weigh more heavy,"** she added. He appeared not to hear as he dropped the second hundredweight in the coal house. **"Hwope 'tis all right, or I zhan't have noo mwore."** With there being only two coal dealers, and the other one disliked by my mam, as was his coal, the complaining seemed pointless.

Having lost my theatre at one end of my bedroom, I occupied myself at the other end. There, from a large box containing a Meccano set, I began construction. Easter at church gave me the idea. As my theatre had been closed, I constructed the closest thing to it, the inside of a church, which it was obvious had much of the theatre about it. I had been told that the drama began there. The words and music of the church were sometimes very beautiful and often moving. Never funny though. "Pity," I thought, "fun would fit well in such a beautiful church as ours."

I planned no production within my church, nor services for that matter. I merely wanted an altar with a cross and candles. These were built of Meccano pieces and all the tiny holes filled with wild flowers. The altar was a chest of drawers, with a quilt as a frontal, and a carpet led up to the sacred spot. Having completed it, I stood back to admire. My mother also looked, and she immediately brought my father to see, saying in a whisper: **"Teake a look at this."** Only once did I see the mixture of bewilderment, shock, admiration and the slightly pale, sick look, as if they were watching a funeral go by. They crept away, saying softly: **"Teake it down when the vlowers do wither,"** and as they went back to their ease: **"Did 'ee ever zee the like?"**

14

"THANK YOU Mrs Waggs, I'm sure you will make a most *eggscellent* substitute."
That was me, addressing the housekeeper, and delivering my first line in my first
school play. Called "Gertie's Ghost," it was a well constructed play, centred on a
boy, small enough to fit into a little cupboard under the stairs, which also
contained the electricity meter. Gerry, the boy, installed there early in the play,
has a great deal of fun making noises, switching lights on and off and, as a final
fling, letting loose a clockwork mouse. I played the Vicar, indeed overplayed it, in
my attempt to extract every ounce of laughter from the part. This was farce – a
school comedy – but real farce. The lights going off is an old farce routine and the
changed positions of the actors, when they come on again, straightforward comic
tableau; the positions being held till the laugh begins to die.

One of the best comic scenes of this nature is the high spot of *Worm's Eye View*
where a team of people are engaged in taking the bulb from the centre light. The
table is being supported, on which a chair is being held, and, reaching from this is
one of the comedy team, shaking with fear. Before reaching the bulb, the light is
switched on by the landlord. The pyramid slips, one of the team landing his foot
in a jelly on the table. At that point the tableau is held. In the first London
production the tableau was held for almost two minutes before the laughter
subsided.

In our little comedy the lights came on and the maid was found in the Vicar's
arms, he, quite liking it, till flooded with light. There was no doubt our play was
the best of the school concert, even the little drama *The Bishop's Candlesticks* came
second to our knockabout farce. My interest in the technical side of the theatre
showed at this early stage. The clockwork mouse could not be relied upon to stop
in the right place, and it was my idea that we used two; one to run across the stage
to – no matter where, and the other to be set where the mother of the family finds
it and proclaims: "Look, it's only a clockwork one." Many 'vicars' followed, but
it was the first that made me feel proud as the audience of parents laughed. The
next year they laughed as I played the Doctor.

"There beant nothen vunny about doctors," said my gran, **"I'd as zoon zee
the butcher come inta house, as the doctor."** Farm-labourers could ill afford
the fees for doctors. Food was more important, though many people were
beginning to think differently. A doctor would not be summoned, unless the
illness was serious. The simple remedies used by country people were no doubt of
some help, but failing to call a doctor because of his fee, led to the unnecessary
advance of some illnesses.

There was a little viciousness in some teachers, I felt quite sure. The bean bag on
the end of a rope helped me to form this opinion. Nothing wrong with a bean bag
at the end of a rope, providing some grinning teacher was not swirling it around
at break-neck speed, as children in a circle round her tried to jump over the rope.
When I was asked to do something, I was generally ready to oblige, when I was
forced, my instinct fought against it. A vicious rope at one's ankles was not the
best way to start a cold Monday morning. Why was it some horrid children knew
when the wretched rope with its bean bag was about to reach them, and were in
mid air as it passed under their feet? Why was it, though I tried, I did not jump
soon enough and collapsed in an untidy heap on the frosty ground, or rose too

soon and then came down, allowing that bag of beans to hit me once again? Had there ever been a report of a teacher being murdered by strangling, that the rope round her neck was pulled tight after she had first been hit over the head with a bag of beans. I would willingly have admitted the crime; willingly and proudly.

Inside, away from the cold and the misnomer "games are good for you" – they fill hospital wards – it was much nicer. In the class-room there was warmth and added to that the *Times Supplement* with its report on India, where it seemed to be hot all the time. Geography of this sort was weighted heavily in favour of the Empire. It presented India as the most romantic place on earth. Excellent pictures of dark-skinned maidens picking tea, with details of the processing to the tasting on a cool verandah. Had I been told that the food I threw to the trout that day would have kept an Indian for a week, now that would have been instruction. Had they added, after saying it was a hot country, that across that vast arid land, lying in deep dust, could be found old men, old women, and young ones, looking old. Had they told of legs and arms with no ends, the frames without limbs and the open sores, those weeping sores, surrounded by flies, had they said a family of sixteen lived in a tent, formed by bent branches and old rags, inside of which, a few pots and pans were their worldly possessions; had they told of that, India would not have been such a shock when I came to know it.

During the hot summer in our Dorset plum orchard, we built our tent, using branches of the trees and old rags. Our play-house was better than the real ones of India and our contents more lavish. Our meals were 'left-overs' from the kitchen. My only complaint within those happy hours of play, was in being called for a meal, when we were in the middle of a meal; ironic compared to a handful of rice. So we stopped in the middle of tea to go for dinner, only to return later for tea and more entertaining hours playing an amalgam of all the fathers and mothers we knew. We emphasized the outstanding features of our models, scandalising the absent Mrs. So and So. The following lines are an attempt to recapture an 'over the garden wall' conversation. It is the dialect spoken during my childhood, which I have set into rhyming couplets.

Between Thee an' I

Dwon't zay I to'd 'ee, will 'ee now?
    But thick dress on the line, I 'llow,
Were bought at last wick's jumble zale,
    I zid'n hangen on the rail.
When I zay, "bought," well thees knoow zhe –
    Noo better than zhe ought t' be.
Zhe measured'n agin 'er lags,
    Then vumbled wi' 'er zhoppen bags;
An' when zhe zid the time was right,
    Zhe popped'n in like, out o' zight.
Vur I did zee thick zelf-zeame dress
    Last zummer, wored be Lady S.
The things zhe buys – I mean zhe teakes –
    Well, when zhe bin t' town, zhe meakes
Out – or tries to – that it be new;

What come ztreaght hwome an' wash 'em drough?
Dost think that be 'is Zunday best?
'Tis vull o' holes, 'er veller's vest.
A ztring woone? well now, there's a thing –
'Oles, tied t'gether wi' zome ztring.
Thick zhirts 'ave zid zome better days,
Zee, zhe's 'angen 'em the wrong ways
Up, vancy putten out they rags –
An' usen they wold gipsy pags.
Nur did zhe wipe along 'er line,
I runs a vlannel wover mine.
Wha's that zhe got, a evenen dress?
Thee's zee ztreaght drough, well mwore or less.
Noo, never; not a neglegee?
Wou's't thee want that, if thees was zhe?
Well, if thees let thee veller zee,
Thee't 'ave a gert big vamily.
'Er zheets be doubled, they'm all catched
Up – done t' hide that they be patched.
Quiet, zhe's comen down the paff,
Zoo, kip a ztreaght veace, dwon'ee laugh.
Good marnen, done yur washen then?
Not yours? oh, you'll 'ang yours out when
Ladyzhip's is dry, I s'ppose
You'm right, zhe 'ave got lovely clwose.

I felt the Holy Spirit descending upon me. A pretentious or a pompous statement? Not really, this was my confirmation. The laying on of hands had occurred and the Bishop of Sherborne, standing in our village church, looked very impressive. Besides I was wearing a brand–new grey flannel suit. Most people will know the feel of new things, but flannel of good quality gives one an elated sensation, at least it did me. Like walking on to a stage in magnificent costume, both for the boys and the girls, so was our confirmation. Added to this the hymn being sung was, 'Our Blessed Redeemer e're He Breathed,' my mother's favourite hymn. Behind me I could hear her familiar voice, a voice which sang with determination rather than grace. I was intoxicated by something, it may have been importance, but I like to think it was the Holy Spirit. Before my reader has a cherub-like image of a saintly boy floating toward the gilt canopy with the dove of peace in its centre, I must tell you of my main thought at that time.

Tommy Trinder had been cracking a gag not so long before, which went something like this:

"There was this vicar y' see. Well, he was waiten for the bishop t' do the confirmation, see, an' he was tellen 'em about the last confirmation like. So, he says, 'All the knobs on the altar rail are holy, 'cos the bishop what come was a bit short sighted.'"

That was the thought in my mind. I also felt a bit guilty, regarding the day before, when I made my confession to our priest. I have not known a more holy man, he was indeed Pastor to us all. Being such a good man, he did the thing that judges warn against in courts of law, he put words into my mouth. "You have done none of these things – there followed a long list – have you Jimmy?" Dare I complicate the issue and single out one or two I had committed, thereby spoiling his view of me? "No," I replied and he smiled. His blessing followed, so I was ready for the Bishop. At the point of kneeling before him, might I have said: "Just a minute, there are one or two things you should know?" Then, spilling the beans on my countless crimes? Should I have said, that because of my erring and straying, my mother had laid hands on me a few times – mainly at the other end – making the impression of her wedding ring show for more serious crimes, and that in view of all this, would he prefer to by-pass the laying on of hands at the top end? "No, I must go through with it." Perhaps it was making that decision that intoxicated me; or was it a feeling of importance after all?

This was an important day, the day on which my mother wore her very best fox fur. They were much worn at that time, though why, it was difficult to understand. Why there should have been weekday furs, Sunday furs and special day furs is beyond my comprehension. The sight of a young well-dressed woman with a fox fur around her neck, especially in the heart of fox country, looked so wrong. My mother disliked the thought of foxes being hunted, and could not bear cruelty to animals, yet there she was with her special fox fur forming a circle round her neck so that its nose and glittery eyes were drawn together with its rear legs and clasped with tassels. The sight seemed to me, inhuman, but not so to the young men who stood around, for want of something better to do. They paid the compliment of a sharp whistle to a **"zmart piece."** She accepted the compliment inwardly, but outwardly her whole being moved briskly ahead, while just her eyes and maybe her chin, moved within the nest of bristling fox fur, as she looked at them with all the contempt she could muster. Such an amount, that I should have preferred not to be on the receiving end.

The older men. Now that was a different story. They said of her: **"Zhe be a zmart piece, and zhe do walk z' good."** Proper carriage and correct walking was important then. **"Ah, if zhe wan't already zpoke vur, I'd be atter zhe,"** came the compliment from a beer-swilling lout, who I would not, in the last resort, have accepted as an alternative father.

Respectability in the village was very important. To be loved was very nice, to be respected, essential. There were rules for respectability, such as, a blue serge suit – but not with brown shoes – sombre ties, short and neat hair and, most important for men, doffing the hat to a lady. Ladies did not have the same rules, it was assumed they would behave. However there was one test for girls. Those who went for country walks with their boy-friends, had to be immaculate on their return. Wrinkled skirts, or a trace of grass on the clothing, brought the remark: **"He do know all about zhe."**

The general test for respectability, was the standard and cleanliness of underwear. **"All top zhow,"** was no good at all, it would have been better to stay at home. Respectable people were very obvious. They were those, who the night before going to town, some nine miles away, bathed and put on clean underclothes in preparation for the trip. **"Well you do never knoow, you mid** [might] **be vound."** To me it seemed as possible to be **found** [knocked down] in the village as, in what surely was the quietest town in Dorset. Walking down the

main street, one could cross and recross the road many times before an Austin
Seven travelled from the Bank to the Cinema, which was all of a hundred and fifty
yards. Still precautions were taken: **"Vur you do never knoow."**

Safe on our side of the road, the Austin Seven trundled by as we gazed at the
placards outside the Tivoli Cinema. A tiny place as buildings go, but a vast place
in its scope for entertainment. Though there was no theatre in the town, the
cinema was a great advance from our once-weekly films in the village. With
continuous performances it was possible to enter at any time, but it was better not
to do so during the 'big' picture. Leading up to that, usually an 'A' category, there
were other short films, plus of course the news.

The cinema flourished in the thirties and standards improved as time went by,
but the American way of life was the basis for many of the screen plays, and alas
Hollywood had a way of giving the saddest story a happy ending. Some of the
stars were those from the silent films, and many of them adapted badly to the
addition of sound. Acting – overacting – as they had in silent days, the screen plays
were more like melodramas, than straight theatre. Those who had worked in the
theatre delivered their lines in the fashion of the actor on a large stage, and the
result was a number of 'corny' scenes, but we loved them all. If Bette Davis was to
play the 'bitch' of the story, how it was done mattered little. We went to see Bette
Davis and she was bound to be good.

Our cinema gave us a view of the stars we loved and eventually it gave us
colour. A musical on film in colour was something to travel for, queue for, and sit
through spellbound, till at last leaving with bleary eyes. Gracie Fields with her
fresh voice, transferred to film and transformed our picture-house into a music-
hall. Gracie, the Lancashire lass, was as English as Greensleeves and she was ours.
From the same county came George Formby with his scratchy humorous voice
which was so infectious. We must not forget this was the period of the banjo, so
George and his ukelele were bound to be popular.

Then came Carmen Miranda, the 'Brazilian Bombshell.' The costumes,
scenery and colour in her films were nothing short of fantastic. Dancing and
swaying her hips in a sensuous way, her eyes flashed enough fire to light the
imagination of her devoted audience. Could I paint, and was asked to produce a
picture showing 'the happiness of living,' I would paint the shades of red which
surrounded Carmen Miranda, culminating in the gorgeous colour of fruit piled
high on her headdress.

English women did not wear hats like that, but they were pretty just the same.
A morning came for my mother to wear her apple-green hat, made up of net and
voile, through which and under the wide brim could be seen a cluster of rose
buds. She clutched her handbag, white gloves and a large bunch of sweet peas, as
I carried her suitcase to the bus. For the first time in my memory she was going
away for a week. I turned from the departing bus, blinded by tears and found my
way home. In my mind's diary there is no entry for that week.

15

THOUGH OUR nearest town boasted a cinema, our village school had no electricity. The light at the end of a dark afternoon came from large oil lamps with massive shades to spread the light over the class-rooms. If we were to be delighted with a series of slides, which we called a magic lantern show, we came back later in the evening when the large windows, which had no blinds, were dark and the oil lantern could be lit. It smoked through a chimney vent in the top and became quite hot, as slide after slide was inserted for our delight. The slides were large glass ones and the whole operation was quite noisy, which was covered by the cheering or booing of excited children.

The operator normally had sets of slides, which gave a complete sequence of an event. A set of Charlie Chaplin slides was the favourite. For example: he waddles into the garden, looks for hosepipe, finds hosepipe, attaches it to the tap, turns on tap, no water comes out, *we* see him standing on hosepipe, he looks down hole from which the water should jet, look of despair, scratches head, looks again, stepping aside, and yes, we had guessed it, a considerable amount of water jets out, as he shows disgust, puzzlement and wonderment, but allowing the jet to remain directed at his face. Yells from all: "Let's see it again." Those early 'picture' shows seem a very long way from the domestic comedy of today's TV.

There were other pictures in that period. No home was a home without pictures. **"Beautiful pictures, they got,"** meant a well furnished country cottage. Over the mantelpiece, each side of the dresser, above those and below, there were pictures, and when the pictures stopped the photographs began. Over the sideboard in our living-room was a large picture in a gilt frame. **"What are they doen?"** I asked my mother. **"They'm angels, one black vur deaf** [death] **and evil and the other white vur good. They'm teaken a zoul t' Heab'm"** [Heaven]. "Indeed," I thought, "if that's going to Heaven, I would rather the other place – or stay here." Each side of that were views of the River Wye – was there ever a wall without the Wye? They were very ordinary prints, but nice in their way. The frames were of cherry wood, but the interesting thing about the pictures, was that a Bournemouth framer tried to keep them after framing, and it took a solicitor's letter to retrieve them. This added to their value, **"Must be wuth** [worth] **a lot, if 'ee wanted 'em,"** as the story was trotted out. **"Now these two be valuable,"** boasted my mother, **"Real oil paintens."** She meant that the originals were valuable and those ordinary copies took on the aura of 'valuable.' **"Zweetly perty wallpaper, and antick** [antique] **pictures"** described the well kept cottage.

"Let me put one of my beautiful combs in your hair," said my sister Iris, and then aside, **"It is filled with poison and she will die."** That is the way she spoke to my younger sister Darthy. When that failed she offered an apple – poisoned of course – and when one bite was taken, Darthy went into a deep sleep and was put into her coffin. So goes my story and that of *The Sleeping Beauty*. Darthy played the Princess, though called Snow White, and Iris played the Witch with a very sinister touch. Played? indeed they were just themselves; even that is not true. On stage they were never as vicious as in real life. Prince Charming was played by a girl, ("Just my luck," exploded Darthy.) and there were seven dwarfs among the other characters. How did seven dwarfs get into the story, or indeed

Snow White? but they were there in the pantomime.

The pantomime played for two nights in the village hall, and knowing Darthy's love of acting, I suspect when the sleeping scene came it was most welcome. I am quite sure by that time, after her singing, "One day my Prince will come," she would have had quite enough of the inane lines specially written for the school production. Real bluebells in the wood scene were effective, but ruined by one of Darthy's little 'boyfriends,' "Mummy, is Dorothy really dead?" I believe Darthy remained 'dead' – I was backstage – but it would have been in character – hers, not the Princess's – for her to have risen up, remove the apple, and exclaim: "No, course not," then put the apple back and recline 'dead.' Darthy was pretty, with ambitions to sing with a dance band. The curtain came down to genuine applause and Darthy made a dash for the girls' dressing room, removing her things and remarking: "Let's get this lot off and get out of here." It was something I could not understand. With half of her popularity I would have stayed till the last light was put out.

The madness of love and passion so often seen in the pantomime story was there in the village and for real. George, a farmer and a recluse was mad, they said, because of thwarted love when he was younger. I saw him rarely and never spoke to him, and that applied to most people, except my mother. She talked to him and seemed to understand his problems. Who the girl in his past was, we were never told, but we did know, because she was 'unobtainable' he became 'the lost soul' we knew. With long hair and an odd grin, he peeped over garden walls and then was lost again for weeks. At his own request he wished to be buried in the village cemetery, though when he died he was many miles from the village. He lies now in the cemetery close to my mother's grave. Still no one knows of his youthful love.

Love has been and always will be, a subject for musicians and writers. Many have tried to define the indefinable. I would not dare to investigate nor produce results on perhaps the most precious thing that humans know. I can only give my childhood impression of love. **"The eyes reveal the soul,"** it is said, and that is a good guide. I think of the Priest from my village, not in his church, chanting, lifting words with much incense, to Heaven. No, I saw him in the street and any other places where villagers gathered, there I saw his eyes. In those eyes were understanding, sympathy, joy, even devilment, but there was more, and that I believe was love. I remember too, an ordinary parishioner, who was the carpenter at the Manor. At our school Christmas party it was his duty, but to him a privilege, to light the many candles on our tall Christmas tree. With a long taper, one by one, the candles were lit, flickering the many coloured reflections from one surface to another. I saw the glowing lights as they increased, but I saw more. His eyes, wide and kindly, reflected all that was Christmas, the colour, the expectation, but, more important, in those eyes was love. Love of duty – an old-fashioned idea to many – the love of Christmas, and, in his surveying of our joyful upturned faces, love for us. Surely love for children at any time, but especially at Christmas, is real love?

Love within a family is one of the oddest things – to a child. The bad language, the squabbling, the bickering and the bitterness displayed are hardly indications of love, yet often that is what they are. Patience is perhaps the basis for love within a family, yet patience is so often tried. My mother lost me my patience on many occasions. She had a habit, which began as a joke, of using the wrong word. Those who follow Hilda Ogden in *Coronation Street* will know how she uses the wrong word, within the character. In her case, she knows no better, but in my mother's it was deliberate and sometimes very humiliating.

"And did zhe insult the doctor?" she might have yelled to a neighbour. **"Consult,"** we whispered. **"I know, consult I meant,"** she said, looking cross, then continuing her yelling, **"When he coulden git her inta hospital, did zhe insult another doctor?"** We gave up, till next time. **"They'm gwoen t' moderate their cottage." "Modernise, mam,"** we hissed. **"Yes modernise, 'twill be lovely when 'tis done; I wish they'd moderate mine."** We were spitting tacks or stamping by now. **"Yes, I remember King Garge's Carnation." "Coronation, Coronation, Coronation, mam." "I yerd 'ee the virst time, yes, Coronation. Talken about carnations, I d' like thick woone y' got in the bworder there. Yes, I d' remember Edward VII's Carnation too."** There was nothing for it but to depart to the river and catch some minnows. One could watch them opening and shutting their mouths. Whether they spoke I do not know, but at least they did not make me cross.

Escape to the river, to the woods, or, if the weather was bad, to my bedroom with a good book. Cronin's *Hatter's Castle* was a good book and a big fat book too. **"Jist right vur keepen a dwoor wopen,"** my mother said, but I tried not to be cross, as it did work very well as a door-stop. However, at that moment I needed the door closed, as I dipped into a few more pages. Perhaps it was the boy being driven to do better at school, till the result of all his study produces failure and ends in stark tragedy, which convinced me that trying too hard only caused problems. That is my explanation, and I intend sticking to it.

I am aware that my lazy attitude at school produced bad examination results, but there is little advantage in being dismal about one's failings, so why not make a feature of them? My normal ability might best be described in that I let a yo-yo run down its string, but often failed to get it to come up again. This, when the very laws of movement ordained that it should. In this period the yo-yo was very popular and was demonstrated as an act in stage shows. Almost every child could be seen playing with one, reeling it down, up, sideways, backwards and even upside down. All except me, and, "My string's snarled." Rotten things anyway, yo-yos, they didn't actually go anywhere or do anything.

At three thirty when the prison doors opened, the frenzied stampede for freedom began. Before that was attained, the school had to say the Lord's Prayer, only at a greater speed than it had been said in the morning. The last line raced out in one long gasp for breath …. ForThineistheKingdomthepowerandtheGlory – foreverandeverAmen – A mad rush for the cloakroom, where the weaker ones were trodden under foot, as the excitement of the day began, conkers!

At the top of the hill there were chestnut trees. Often a number of the green-husked nuts were blown down, but the better ones had to be knocked down by throwing large sticks. "Watch out," as the stick, plus conkers landed on another's head. Pockets stuffed with both sorts of chestnuts and mouths crammed with the sweet variety, though being unripe they had a bitter taste, we made our way down the hill to the village shop, to buy at least one firework and to envy the rockets and little demons. Sparklers were cheap, but regarded as rather cissy. After all, one could only stand and hold the thing, till it fizzled out. They never actually *did* anything. Nature must have designed sweet chestnuts, so that boys would be too full to think of sweets, when the important business of choosing fireworks was dominant in our minds.

How can I describe our village shop? it almost defies description. Where to begin, that is the problem? I have thought about it and describe it as homely, very inefficient, but homely. Had you been there that day, I could not have asked you in, for six boys, many boxes, empty and half full, tins, jars, bottles and bags took up most of the floor space. The remainder boasted a chair upon which a dear old lady had settled for a bit of peace. I felt she would have done better staying at home. The counter, we assumed there was one, for no living person had seen it in enough detail to recognise it in a court of law, was covered by layer upon layer of odd things. It was the juxtaposition of items which astounded. Butter, with a wire for cutting, and loose pepper spilling nearby. Cheese in the round, from which some cuts had been made, and over it were several sets of men's braces. Odd quarters of tea and half pounds of marge were strewn among blue bags; blue bags half filled with sugar, blue bags half filled with currants, blue bags semi-filled with rice and blue bags – just blue bags, littering an area of assumed counter and floor space.

Behind all that was order – apparent order. There, in labelled drawers were many things, or so the customer imagined. Alas most of the items from those drawers were spread around the shop. I pointed to a particular drawer and said **"Mam told me to get some cloves,"** pleased to have remembered. The shopkeeper was jovial, buxom, lovable, gossipy, but not too clean a woman. Peering over her rather grimy gold-rimmed bifocals, she pondered: **"Cloves, now let me see, am I expecting them in, or have I only just ordered them, or are they under there?"** 'Under there,' was below the huge pile of jumbled items on the floor. **"If they'm under there, then you tell yur mam we han't got any,"** she laughed. No cloves? when I had remembered, was a distaster, they would never believe me at home. Then, lifting a piece of greaseproof paper which had been used for totting up on, she found a scoop half filled with cloves. With a squeal of laughter – she laughed at triumph or disaster – she began to look for a bag. In the disorder I knew where they were. They were the same as sweet bags, under the end of a side of bacon, that is where they were. Success, well almost.

The two ounce weight was 'under there somewhere,' so four ounces it had to be. **"Mam said, put 'em on the book please,"** I told her and she began to look for a pencil. I knew where that was, though her hair had fallen down on one side, it was tucked behind her ear. Much laughter in the discovery of it, and the fact that it had no point, then – as you may have guessed – the search for a knife to sharpen the pencil. Luckily the fireworks were in the window, even more lucky, she had no idea of the price of little demons – but I did. Laughter followed us from the shop – our sniggers were suppressed – as we dragged the door to and the bell jangled because the door hit a bump in the floor. My mother said: **"Where have you bin all this time?"** and I answered, **"Getting your cloves mam."** She smiled: **"Who's a thoughtvul bwoy then?"** to which I knew the reply: **"I am mam."**

A hurried tea, for the night that followed, was social night. In the village hall there was to be fun and games and all sorts of turns on the stage. There was the funny story told time and time again, till all knew it by heart. Two Grammar

School boys slipped back into their Dorset accents to tell the time-worn story. It demonstrates the rather dry sense of humour to be found in Dorset and the delight in the dialect, both for the story-teller and the listener. I still find joy in the story with its familiar punch-line. So the boys began in their 'posh' voices:

> *Two farmers meet one morning.* [taking it in turns with the dialect]
> **"Good marnen Garge."**
> **"Good marnen Jake."**
> J: **"Wha's 'ee gi'** [give] **thy hoss** [horse] **when 'ee had the hump?"**
> G: **"I gid'n** [gave him] **turkumtine.** [turpentine].
> J: **"Did 'ee Garge?"**
> G: **"Ah Jake."**
> **"Good marnen Garge."**
> **"Good marnen Jake."**
>
> *The two farmers meet again next day at about the same time.*
> **"Good marnen Garge."**
> **"Good marnen Jake."**
> J: **"Wha's 'ee zay thee gi' thy hoss when 'ee had the hump?"**
> G: **"I zaid I gid'n turkumtine."**
> J: **"Well, I gid my turkumtine an' 'ee died ..."** [pause]
> G: **"Ah, zoo did mine."**

We laughed at them, at ourselves and at the slowness of the humour. There were those in educational fields who thought the dialect/accent should be discouraged. Those same people admired the north country dialects, which left me wondering, are we ashamed of our own? Perhaps there should have been a law to preserve our speech. Laws are made in Parliament and many in the village thought, **"They lot zhould be blowed up."** Guy Fawkes failed to do that, which gave us the opportunity to burn him on a magnificent bonfire each fifth of November. The joy of darkness, out of which rose pure magic in the coloured stars of rockets, was the most exciting time between Harvest and Christmas. More pleasurable than the cries of delight from children were the sounds of adults being children all over again. I think of the lady who yelled: **"Ooh, that was a good'n."** At church on Sunday she read what sounded like: **"The Gauspel accauding to St Look."** We aped her then: I do so now: **"Hea endeth the fifteenth chapta."**

16

THE RIVER Allen claimed so much of my attention, but I do not regret spending much of my childhood at its edges, and it was most welcome when it crept into the bottom of our garden. Not many had a private sea in their garden. The river played an important part in my upbringing, so perhaps tragedy was inevitable as experience of life at an early age. I loved the river, but did not forgive it claiming a little school friend. **"Jist eight,"** they said, **"And his wonly child."** A few miles down river she had fallen in and the current carried her body some miles to a bridge, where she was found a week later. The first experience of a friend dying is bound to have considerable effect, and produce the stock complaint: **"Why, why, why? life is so unfair."** Some people said: **"Zhe bin took, 'cos zhe be z' good. God do want her vur His."** I did not, nor do I believe God works in that way. Some children from the school formed a small choir in order to sing our little friend's favourite hymn, the first verse of which has always stayed in my mind:

"As pants the hart for cooling streams
  When heated in the chase,
So longs my soul, O God, for thee,
  And thy refreshing grace."

I believe sad events stick in the mind more firmly than the happy ones. The tune of that hymn will always bring to mind a bereaved father, bowed and broken. He, who had been robust, cheerful and always ready with a joke, could not lift his head, as tears rolled down his cheeks. It was rare to see a man cry – the stiff upper lip was firmly taught – and it left a lasting impression. I was shocked by his tears, but saw no shame in his face.

"Work do take yur mind off things," they said. Not good advice to those who had little else to think about but work. My father worked hard, and never harder than when **drashen** [threshing]. The threshing machine pulled between two ricks, where, stationary, it did the job that the combine harvester does today. My father 'fed' the machine on its platform. Cutting the **string** [binder twine] from each sheaf of corn, he fed them into the drum, which grasped them and the sorting of grain from chaff began. The **smeech** [dust] needs to be seen on a sweating face, to be believed. As a boy I could barely stand a few moments in the black dust. No wonder at the end of a **drashen day,** the labourers looked wild, tired and disheartened by their lot.

Monday was the normal washday, but during threshing time there would be additional washing sessions. At the back of the bungalow was a lean-to shed with a galvanised roof, and in the corner a large copper, under which a wood-burning fire was lit to do the 'whites' boil. The whole of Monday was given over to washing. The pre-wash was done with hard household soap, before boiling and a blue bag was used for the final whites dip. The blue bag was also kept at hand for bee, **wops** [wasp] or ant stings. Just another part of the washing ritual was the starching of shirts, collars, cuffs, tablecloths and anything else that needed to appear crisp and fresh. Washday was a very long day, and most of it was spent under the galvanised roof, which dripped water from the condensed steam. There could be no sigh of relief, for when it had all been brought in from the drying lines **"I think 'tis zpitten wi' rain,"** there was a huge mound of ironing to be done.

Ironing was accomplished with a series of flat irons placed in front of a good red-hot coal fire of a kitchen range or grate, and used in turn, often producing better results than many modern electric irons.

Besides the normal family wash, there were items which very few women would bother with today. Bolster covers, for instance, which were placed below the pillows, valances around the base of the bed and various loose covers and cloths for protecting tables and chairs. A woman was judged by her washing. Is it new? Is it good? Is it **"well looked after"** [neatly mended]? and, most important, is it well washed? The final accolade went to the woman who washed and ironed in one day. That, with her normal day's work meant going to bed very tired indeed. Most children and surely all fathers hated washdays. There was nothing much to be gained from washing faces, hands, or for that matter, things.

The same copper boiled three large Christmas puddings in October or November and the lead-up to that was much more interesting. All those fascinating things in blue bags. Surely no harm could come from just a peep? I was mistaken, a slapped hand was the signal to wait for a particular bag to be opened. Even chopped suet was nice to a hungry child – but it was bag opening time. Currants – **"Hands off, they han't bin washed yet"** – currants are rather small and a few went nowhere at all in the hungry little hole before dinner time. Sultanas, now that was better, some of those went further. There was a bag with sugar, and another bag with different sugar and, at last, there was the bag I had waited for. **"Woone piece wonly, an' keep yer hands out o' the bag."** They often say mothers need the eyes of a hawk. I have news for you, my mother had such eyes, what is more she had the hawk's wing-power in her arms, and surely her long fingered hands were as talons? they certainly gripped that way. That last bag contained candied peel; "Rather wasted in puddings," I thought. Silver threepenny bits in each pudding was a thrilling thought, but the long topping-up with boiling water through the day, most uninteresting. After all, I had helped with the stirring!

I had thought by dwelling on the nicer things, I might blot out the memory of the nastier. Moving into the top class and to the Headmaster was something I had dreaded. Five per cent of the time he was the most attractive and imaginative man. His appreciation of the arts, his sense of humour and his ability to think as a boy again, were things that seemed to get lost ninety-five per cent of the time. Pause to check: 5 plus 95 = 100%, correct. With his powerful influence still around, it is best to be sure. He had the sharp nose of the mathematician, the cutting tone of a Member of Parliament – in opposition and the aggression of a toreador about to sink the blade.

When the day began with his wearing of gold-rimmed *pince-nez,* it meant his temper was already frayed. Watching the gold chain falling in a loop and wobbling as he screeched chalk at speed across the black-board, one knew he waited, as does a hungry tiger, for some stupid boy to fray his temper just a little further. Foolhardy as I often was, I would not have tempted him in that condition. If the humour lines showed around his eyes and mouth, that he had recently laughed, then I might have goaded him. His brow was furrowed and his normally sleek hair, sticking up at the back. That day was not a goading day.

Silence is the blankness in a noisy child's life, and in the end of term exams I experienced both. Blank paper, nice new pens and pencils and, an almost alien teacher: "You have one hour. If you cannot complete a question go to the next, then if you have time, return to the others. [Wait for it.] Begin." Then began the silence and the blankness. The infants were singing, "Oh the merry month is leafy June," through the wall. In any case it was late March and not a very merry March at that. A toddler was running across the playground to the lav. Freedom; could I? no, I had just been. Not feeling very well? perfectly well–just blank. What did he say? "We have touched on every subject in the paper." Ah well, here goes. Say what you know of tea production. Dare I say: "Mam produces it when the kettle boils, then puts four spoons in and one for the pot?" That is all I really wished to know about tea. "No, I must try," I thought– "or go to the next one." "Time; put your pens down." I had thought he would never say it, yet still hoped he would not. I wondered why he took a second look at mine when he picked it up and then screwed up his nose.

If there had been reasonable questions, like, "How many beech trees in the spinney across the field from the school?" I could have answered, and told him some interesting things about them. Who wanted to know abut tea? The beeches were worth studying at any season, especially the smoothness and flatness of their boughs, the grace of their stature, the distribution of limbs, and the peace of mind they gave to those who loved them. The Head was a keen follower of Hardy, though he rarely mentioned Williams Barnes. It was he who loved the beech trees and wrote about them in his poetry. Like him, I looked back sadly at my beeches when I wrote my poem in the Dorset dialect.

The Beech Bough

They didden zay the wold beech bough
'Ould be too ne'r the groun' t' 'llow
O' me t' zwing;
Nur did they zay that all the geames
Be thick girt tree, like carven neames,
An' everything

Were lost, 'ould never come agean
Not even ztrollen down the leane,
A-drough the dust;
An' whittlen o' a grean ash ztick,
Or climben o' a girt thatched rick;
That, end it must.

They didden zay we'd grow zome day,
Git wolder, wiser, goo away
T' dream zomewher'
Alwone, wi' mid be thousands mwore,
Replacen myriads gone avore,
Yet, dreamen yer.

Nur did they zay, woone day the view,
Wi' noo beech leaves vur looken drough,
'Ould be z' bare:
There 'oulden be noo Rwoman moun's,
Vur 'zhadowen the zunlit downs,
An' tidden vair.

They didden zay how little bwoys
Do grown away an' leave their twoys,
An' thick beech bough;
We didden knoow the world mid call,
Not 'llowen dreamers yer at all;
But knoow it now.

My fondness for the beeches went with my love for the people who strolled beneath them. A stroll on a sunny afternoon and home for tea, tea with a background of the Dorset dialect was the most relaxing experience. **"Butter do goo mad twice a ye'r,"** [year] describes it being hard in the winter and soft in the summer [even on the cold flagstones of the larder]. In my mind's eye I can still see a country woman cutting a cottage loaf, which looked so difficult, but was second nature to the cottager. The loaf was held against the stomach with one hand, while the other held a very sharp knife [carver and not a saw] to cut each slice. My grandmother sat to do this, giving the impression of playing a cello, but most women stood for the operation. Seeing the loaf resting on the stomach, simplified the observation: **"I knew that avore yer mother was cutten bread on y'."**

The real joy of the dialect for me is the villager observing; here the stranger might be a little lost. Spars in Dorset are pointed hazel sticks, which are cut and bent, much like a hair pin, and they are driven into the thatch of a roof to keep it in place. Spars are also sparrows. With this in mind, it was possible to hear: **"The spars be pullen the thatch out, zoo we must git zome mwore spars, zoo they dwon't pull out noo mwore."** Conversations heard from a distance and out of context are perhaps the best. In a discussion with a woman on the subject of vegetables for dinner, I heard my mother **hawking** [calling] to her:

"Ould 'ee like a mar vur t'mar?"
"Would you like a marrow for tomorrow?"

Most strange they have found it, yet to me, warm, lovable, homely and very precious. Childhood lingers in the sound of the dialect and the emotional link is strong. Today, if I wish to make an observation to myself, I do it in dialect, which might be as follows:

Now, this is the problem [in standard English].
"I z'pwose I mid do that, but on 't'other hand, I midden [might not].
"Wuth [worth] **gi'en** [giving] **it a try. Ah, I reckons I zhall.**
Decision made. Good ... [in standard English]

If, as is often the case, I can find no answer, I resort to my father's conclusion:
"Well, there 'tis an' can't be noo 'tisser."
The emotional link is obvious in illness. I might have felt happier with:

"How do 'ee veel? boun' t' git wuss [worse] **'vor it do git better."**

The following might have **"put me back a bit"**:

"Oh you're looking awfully seedy, but one can feel worse when recuperating."

Then, it is assumed those sort of people would never have understood an older villager who told the doctor: **"I be queer, zoo me wife did zay I better come t' zee 'ee about it."**

"I do veel zhaky," said my father, as if he had come face to face with his own ghost. He was perfectly sober and had walked home across the field and down through the garden to our back door. It took a little time to gather what the problem was. **"'Twas evil, evil, evil,"** he repeated. He had passed the dew pond, which was grown over with grass, but still a deep hollow. In the bottom was some water and old leaves. **"Zparks, zparks an' vire,"** he said, still shaking. Tradition had it that this 'sparking' was the work of the devil, and worse, it was only attracted to evil people. My father may have had his bad moments, but could not have been described as evil. His horror, was not so much the seeing, but in being 'chased' by the fire. I quote this, so that the reader can compare with similar phenomena occurring in other parts of the country. The marshes of the East coast come to mind, where the marsh gases could produce a similar effect. In my part of Dorset it was the most sinister thing possible, with none of the fairy-tale dimensions of will-o-the-wisp.

Evil, wicked, the latter word was used for anything distasteful. **"Wicked,"** was how some described Mrs Simpson when her name was linked with King Edward VIII, **"a divorced woman, marry our King, never."** Our village church would not have been the scene of a divorced person's marriage, so it was difficult to see the King involved in such a union. There were those in the village however, including my mother, who said: **"If he d' love her, he zhould be 'llowed t' marry her."** Abdication was a word almost unknown in our circles till then, but it was on most people's lips. There were wicked stories, there were silly stories and there were moving stories of their romance. The general opinion seemed to be that even had Mrs Simpson designs on the British Throne, in that she wished to be Queen, they should be allowed to marry. They were of course allowed to marry, but not as King and Queen. The moving abdication speech will be forever in many minds. The words were repeated in my village and throughout the land. Any man in the village, faced with the same problem might have said: **"I can't do me work wi'out thick 'oman I do love a-zide o' me."**

Our Royal family had to set the example for others, but when the decision is made to 'opt out' of any family 'for love' it is to be hoped that later there are no regrets. My maternal grandfather was a farmer's son, but because he married a 'factory girl' he was 'locked out' of the family. He returned to the farm as a labourer, but unlike the Prodigal, there was no fatted calf. Family life can be difficult, whether Royal or common and even at the age of eleven, I was aware of the double standards in public life. It seemed to me we were taught, "Love and forgive as God forgives – but we will have no loving or forgiving here in our church, or for that matter in Westminster Abbey."

17

I LOVED her deeply, a secret passionate love that grew day by day. Our eyes met while we were engaged in the simplest tasks and an understanding passed between us. In laughter, in study, in difficulties, in everything we were together, ticking as two clocks set in exactly the same way. Her eyes had the riveting smile of a conqueror, yet why I do not know, for there never was a battle. I knew there was another to whom she was devoted, but that was a poorer relationship than the one which held us together. Instinct shows the way for true love, words or actions are unnecessary. The only problem with unspoken love, is when one partner turns to others, even if formal politeness demands it, there can be no commanding the wanderer to return. She danced, she sang, but above all she was an actress. Her heroine to my hero was a dream and in my dreaming the days passed quickly. When the school day ended, life was duller. The world without that strong personality was as cold as a field of green corn without the sun. I wrote secret poems, and I now reveal one of them.

First Love

You showed me poise and grace and taught me how to look,
How to listen, how to talk, and how to read a book.
Leaning over, held my hand, and guided it to draw,
Called me by my Christian name, and gave me Christian law.
In return I give my heart, are you aware of this?
You call me and I answer, but alas – just "Miss."
But you have forty other loves, and as the school year starts,
Former forty move with broken pencils – broken hearts.
You taught me how to do my sums, and do my sums I can,
Forty times forty jilted loves in your teaching span.
Oh story-telling brazen hussy, do you really care?
With steady gaze you answer, "Yes," no other could I bear.
To turn your head I raise my hand, hear me calling, "Miss,"
Give me your reassuring smile – for all I need is this.

I never saw her as the Headmaster's wife, as our relationship was on a much higher plane than, "Will you have tea in your study, in the dining room, or the kitchen?" They had other rooms too, and she may have been his in any of them, that was their affair. Ours was the garden, a sloping-lawned pleasure of a garden. The Head kept it in good order and having mowed the lawn, he departed to tend his bees in their hives, beyond the shrubs and out of view. He kept an excellent garden, and went away leaving it to the non-practical, the artists, to enjoy.

The freedom of that garden is difficult to describe. It was her presence, and her artistic ability, that enhanced the colours and scent of the flowers, the pile of the carpet of lawn and even the warmth of the sun on relaxed limbs. What were we doing in the garden? Were we with others or alone? Alone, apart from thirty girls in green dresses, taking their positions for country dancing, and they could be ignored. They merely acted upon the orders of their Priestess – my Goddess. She, the choreographer, and I the orchestra, as at her command I played a sort of musical robot. She had asked her husband for my services – he did not suspect, or dare refuse – and, free of the class-room, I carried the portable gramophone and a pile of records to the lawn, where I set them in order and awaited her instructions.

Leaning there on the warm grass, watching a new dance take shape in front of the blazing colour of the flowers, I knew happiness. We were artists, she and I, as I watched her blue eyes under the blue of a perfect sky, but more, we were technicians, she knowing every step required, and I knowing each groove of every record. "Shall we go back ... " and I was ready before she spoke to her dancers. "One, two, three, four," she demonstrated, and I hit the spot on the record. Her husband may have been Headmaster, clever with sums, gardening, bees and the intimate side of married life, but he could not have known the emotional intensity of an artistic relationship.

From a beautiful relationship to the marriage of my sister Iris – to me! There was little artistry about the way they dressed us, she in her veil and long dress, I in topper and tails, with a bow tie made of silver paper. Waiting on the green outside the church, I feared for my bow tie and prayed it would stay intact till the ceremony was over. The band played, the maids of honour led the way, and following, we went hand in hand around the village. I disliked shows in the open air, especially unrehearsed ones, with all that might go wrong. I longed for the end of the procession, when our priest would pronounce – the winners of the fancy dress competition.

This was Coronation Day, the Coronation of King George VI in 1937. It was a strange sensation, moving around the village among a number of familiar people, all in fancy dress. Stranger, seeing decorations among the wild grass of the banks. Little arches of red, white and blue, old flags and new ones hanging from windows, plus the farm wagons bedecked with bunting and flowers. I had never seen horses or wagons so decorated. **"'Tis woonce in lifetime,"** they said. **"Ah,"** said my mother. **"'Ee dwon't zee many Carnations."** "Coronations," we whispered, **"Ah, Coronations. The last time the village looked s' nice 'twere King Garge V's Jubilee. Ah, it mid** [might] **be a long time avore we d' zee another Carnation."** A Monarch becomes very familiar, and it seemed strange to be singing "God save the King" – a new King. Iris and I won first prize which made it all much less strange.

First prize in the shape of money was well worth all the effort, and our parents had worked hard on our entry in the fancy dress competition. **"'Tis nice,"** said my mother, **"That we won a prize."** Had we not, the story would have been different. **"Tidden vair, zhan't enter agean; course we midden** [might not] **be yer vur next Carnation,"** she predicted. **"Coronation, mam,"** we hissed. **"Ah, Coronation, wonly the Lard d' knoow if we shall be yer vur another Carnation."** Fancy dress to my mother was **"Jist vur vun."** Anything done in an amateur sense, was close to being stupid. Her lines were straight and narrow, black and white and quite definitely professional rather than amateur. She spoke of the first with all the reverence reserved for the Pope, the second with all the disdain poured on he who held a tennis racket the wrong way and rarely returned the ball; that was, and is, me.

The sharp differences marked by my mother, were common to country people. Their sense of values was often aimed at heights they might not attain. It was no use anyone being proud of rolled gold, it needed to be 18 carat for my mother to take an interest. She scoffed at 'good cut glass' and called it paste. There was a vogue at that time for strings of pearls, and if they were said to be graduated, it gave the impression of being hand-picked. "Graduated," coaxed the salesman, "But imitation," scorned my mother. As for costume jewellery; if said slowly with a tight-lipped sneer on 'costume,' you will get the tone. In the same class were 'Made in Hong Kong' and 'Made in Germany.' Though my parents added: **"Clever buggers, the Germans."**

"Got they vur vighten the Germans," said my father. In a side table drawer were his medals from the 1914–18 war. The medals lay in the drawer gathering dust, together with a bicycle puncture repair outfit, a spanner and a winder for bed springs. The sight of the decorations, so pushed away, depressed me. They were made to be worn with pride, not stored away in a dusty drawer. Medals, like photographs, should be treasured or destroyed, otherwise they demean the cause or the sitter.

Who am I to talk of respect? Did I have proper respect for my dear friend's resting place? She was a tabby cat and in her old age, caught cat 'flu and died in a few days. In a shoe box I buried her, together with her saucer, saying some words over her; at least I said, "Ashes to ashes, dust to dust," before the interment. I carved suitable words on a brush stand, which minus the hooks, made a good tombstone. "Where is the lack of respect?" you may ask. I will explain that my behaviour was right and proper to a time some three months later, when I dug her up to "see how she was getting on." My mother was very cross, and said: **"You'm unkind, how would you like to be dug up?"** I got her point, but we both knew she had expressed it badly.

Many will be taken back to their childhood when hearing the call: **"Go in quickly, it's raining."** You will have gathered my childhood and my mother, who was in part responsible for it, were very perverse. **"Goo on in quick, vur the sun be zhinen."** How much more perverse could one become? The explanation is simple, simple in all its complications. The front windows of the bungalow faced south, they were large windows, and had roller blinds, behind which were fine patterned lace curtains – for peeping through. **"The zun do ztrike hot,"** my mother had said, so down came the blinds. All done? Not by any means. There were prize plants on the window-sills which must be taken to a shaded area of the room. On the settee and easy chairs were silk embroidered cushions and there were other more ordinary cushions which must be placed on top of the better ones. With that done, had we reached the end? oh no, on the back of the settee and the arms of the easy chairs, were linen covers. Prettily embroidered though they were, they had to be placed on top of the poorer cushions. Done? not yet, over all that went several sheets of newspaper. **"The ztrong zun do veade zoo,"** she whispered, as if the contents of a volcano approached.

"Ooh dear, that woon't do at all," my mother complained. A flower pot in an ornate jardiniere had been placed on the polished top of an oval gate-legged table, and the procedure for doing that was as follows: first a lace mat, to save scratching the table. Upon this a round silver card – from the base of a wedding cake – then an embroidered doiley, and, please believe me, then a piece of paper to preserve the doiley. Finished? dear me no. Newspaper was spread over the table **"T' ztop the zun teaken the polish out."** That must have been the end, with the room dark, cool – and covered?

"Jist a mo'," said my mother, as she scurried for more newspaper. In the corner, under a picture of Wells Cathedral, which was a photograph taken from Tor Hill – I though tor *was* a hill – was an Edwardian chair covered in red velvet. Already covered by a large lace cloth, on top of which was a piece of fawn linen – in case someone sat on it – a large piece of newspaper was needed to cover it – though in a part of the room dark with shade – because, **"'Tis better t' be zeafe than zorry."** Brass fire irons shone in front of a much-shined fireplace. It had been out of use for days, with all its surfaces grate-blacked. I might have wished you had been there to see it, but of course that would not have been possible, for layers of newspaper concealed the results of all that polishing, **"Jist in cease the zoot d' vall."** The room was closed off from the sun – **"Tha's wonly a cheap rug, but 'twould be a pity t' veade'n,"** said my mother, finally closing it from the sun, and with the front step too white to be trodden on, from human habitation as well. With its flowers in position, the room might have been a tomb or shrine, the pictures of angels and the Madonna supported that impression. The room was so much better in the winter, most rooms are, especially when they become a little untidy.

Winter in that room, by the light of a tall Victorian oil lamp, which helped to warm the room, was pleasant. Simple, homely and pleasant. A large cloth over the table, and out came all the bits and pieces of a child's collection. Three children using one table led to problems, which sometimes ended with a pushing match to regain original space or to take a little more for the paint box. (This must have been how wars began). **"Mam, she's pinched my brush." "Tidden yours, it's mine,"** and so on. My darning mother, pretending not to be aware, could stop it all with one look. If it had been a Monday night, we behaved, because Mondays were special. We had a new wireless, one on which it was possible to get several foreign stations, but, **"Dwon't you dare touch."** Monday night had been in our minds for a week, and there we sat glued to our wireless for *Monday Night at Eight.* Silence came down at its beginning and endured till the end of the programme – they were listening days. The 'jingle' was not unlike the concert party chorus:

"It's Monday night at eight o'clock,
And can't you hear the chimes, ..."

We listened avidly, waiting for "Puzzle Corner," had a small supper and went happily to bed. It had been a tremendous evening. Snug in bed, the line of a Scottish song we were learning came to mind:

"While ye were sleepen on your pillows,
Thought ye not of our poor fellows?"

..... and though we had no family or friends who were fishing on the high seas, we did know the shepherd and it was lambing time. Out there on the cold windy down he was struggling to help the **yows** [ewes] bring their lambs into the world. A shelter of hurdles, covered by straw, had been erected by my father, who was the farm's thatcher – and the best for miles. The large pen of half thatched shelters looked not unlike the stockades of the wild west. Nearby was the shepherd's caravan. With its little stove, it was a very welcome haven in the early hours of the morning. Poets have always written of caravans, and understandably, for there was great security in that van under the pine trees. On a cold winter's day, as the wind bit its way across the down, I watched the sheep with their shepherd, and thought of those shepherds at Christmas long ago. Some years later, using as a base, St Luke's Gospel, I wrote my poem. My thought was that our shepherd was very close to the real Christmas out there on the Dorset Downs.

St Luke's Story of Christmas

[According to a Dorset Man]

Now Zaeser never did relax
The laws o' they in Galilee;
Zoo Jozeph gooes t' pay 'is tax,
As was wrote down in the decree.
   He journeyed drough the country wild,
    Wi' 'is wife Meary, gert wi' child.

An' zoo it was, when they was there –
Vur zhe 'ould be delivered zoon –
They voun' a loawly zteable bare,
Lit wonly be the ztars an' moon.
   An' the oxen weren't noo deanger,
    Vur they let 'em use the meanger.

The zheep were not zoo vur away,
Wi' zhepherds, biden in the night;
The ztars were zheenen jist like day,
An eangel come down wi' mwore light.
   An' when they zid the glow 'ee meade,
    They, all o' 'em, were zore avread.

But thick grand eangel were quite kind,
Zaid: "Vear not, goo wi' woone accard
T' Diavid's Zity, Thees'll vind
A Zeaviour, who be Christ the Lard;
   An' I t' thee this zign do give,
    Thick Child be barn that men might live."

Zhepherds, down on knees a-prayen,
Vur they were terr'ble vrightened, when
Other eangels come down zayen,
"Peace on earth, good will t' men."
   Then all the eangels in the zky
    Zang: "Glory be t' God on 'igh."

An' when the eangels went vrom them,
They did zay woone to another,
"We'd better goo t' Bethlehem,
Vind 'im, Jozeph, and 'is Mother."
  As zoon as they the beaby zees,
  Vell down 'avore 'im on their knees.

It zimmed as if the beaby zmiled,
An' they zmiled back, which did zim right;
They zaid: "We'll tell about the Child
That we 'ave zid this Hwoly night."
  But Meary knew the Mother's part,
  An' pondered these things in her heart.

Wimborne St Giles: the stocks

18

"I BE a-walken t' Zal'sbury," the old man said, "An' wants t' be there be nightvall." He was one of the many tramps who came through the village. These were the days before the Social Security Service, and the place for down-and-outs was the Union or Workhouse. In most towns there was a Union, which today might be a free hostel, or a bed for the night. Next day, the walk to the next town, with stops at the villages in between. One of the oddest, yet moving expressions I knew, was that on the face of a housewife, working in the kitchen, with food on show, and in view of a tired and hungry old man, who had yet to walk fourteen miles to the next town. She asked herself: "Was he a genuine tramp? Was he a young crook pretending to look old and tired? Ask him into the kitchen in that state? Tell him to go away? No, that could not be done. Cut him some sandwiches and make him some tea?" All of which time he would be at the kitchen door, or worse in the kitchen. A tramp, a rather smelly tramp, close to the kitchen table was not a recipe for relaxation.

My mother's face would have gone through the gammut of emotions before reaching her decision. "You goo an' zit in the zun," [it began to rain] "An' I'll bring 'ee zome vood an' drink" [which meant I would take it]. On delivering a half a loaf of bread and a hunk of cheese, I felt reasonably happy, but on giving him a chunk of butter, which he looked at with open mouth, meaning he had nothing with which to spread it, defeated the suspicion of a concealed knife; but in spite of that he was not given a knife. I felt better when I took him his can of tea, a blue enamel can with a lid in the shape of a cup and used as his drinking vessel. I wondered whether we should have done more, though thought of a much used expression: "Half a lwoaf is better than nwone."

"Two hids [heads] be better than woone [one], even if 'tis wonly a zheep's hid." said my mother. This meant that she had hit on an idea, excusing it as being arrived at by another's thought as well, when in fact, it was quite the reverse. "Time yer kitchen chimley [chimney] was zwept," said a local lad, needing a couple of bob. "I'll think about it," my mother replied.

She had thought and preparations were under way in the kitchen. Everything was moved back from the range and all other furniture covered with dust sheets. Taking a long pole, she tied a clump of newspaper to the top, then when it had been saturated with paraffin, she lit it and pushed it up the chimney. After a short while the stick was retrieved and hidden. Hiding the stick – the evidence – was important. Then she prepared for another of her performances. "Now," she said, "I'm ready." Opening the back door, she ran into the garden, shouting for the benefit of all, "Me chimley's on vire, me chimley's on vire." The neighbours, concerned, were told not to bother with the fire-brigade – as they would discover the offence of setting a chimney alight. "'Tis avire, but quite zeafe," she said. All went back to their houses mumbling: "Mother Attwell zeaven a couple o' zhillen agean."

"I enjäy a good vire," said my mother. I enjoyed a good fire, in the right place and at the right time. However, the roar of flames in the chimney and belching smoke across the village made me feel very insecure. The kitchen was nicer the next day, with its scrubbed table, scrubbed white over the years. "You can eat off'n" [without plates], was the boast. The dresser's ware [crockery] washed and shining, the coconut mats taken up, cleaned and reversed, then replaced on layers of clean newspaper to catch the dust. The pieces of lino, bought at the door for a few coppers, had been washed and the oddness of the different patterns showed up more brightly, except where, over the years, the lino had worn into the square brick tiles beneath it. On the scrubbed table, a cottage loaf – a crusty one, a dish of butter with a jug of milk, both from the farm, and, the thing I still dream about, or wake up in the night wishing I had; home-made blackcurrant jam. Perhaps it is the 'bitter-sweet' of memory, but the taste of such jam today would re-awaken all the love in me for a spot which some called a **"God vorzaken hole,"** but to me was the place of my upbringing and therefore part of me.

"God vorzaken hole," indeed, we even had Italian opera. On a hot sunny afternoon, lying in the long grass of the mead, looking up at the sky and trying to discern a skylark, while being serenaded with the waltz theme from *Traviata,* was not being forsaken. The music in the distance sounded better than on the gramophone. It came from a street organ, and there is no tone quite like that – except perhaps the piano in the infants' class at our school. In many people's minds the street organ goes with city streets, where they were so common in Victorian and Edwardian times, but they were common enough in our village. We did not run to see them, as we might have done for an airship. Perhaps it was the bass notes of the street organ that were so attractive. Certainly they were fascinating, possibly because they were mechanical.

Glorious is the only word I can use to describe the mechanical music of the steam roundabout. Organ, trumpets, drums and whistles, all crashed through the sunny afternoon to delight the once-a-year listeners. All a child's listening and all his viewing needed to be concentrated on this. The flower-show was the first attraction, but that may be summed up as lots and lots of flowers and vegetables set out in rows. Boring old things, all of which could have been seen at anytime. I cared not who had the biggest or best, the best was just beyond the trees. The mystery, the excitement, the brashness, the sheer 'gipsyness' of it all was compelling.

Was that a shaft of sunlight through the trees, or the glint of brass? The hiss of steam was there and the power of the engines, massive, ornate, as though designed for a palace yard, rather than a village field. Solid brass, rounded brass, edgings of brass and those enchanting barley twists of brass. So far we had only viewed the engines, the power that would drive our dreamland later in the night, when, with strings of coloured lights, a field would be a world of fantasy. The Victorians knew how to satisfy greedy eyes. Theatres and fairgrounds were places where their artists came into their own. Perhaps those who went to fairs needed to **"Live like Lords"** just for a few hours, certainly the designers must have had this in mind. They painted marble effects in numerous shades, they painted boldly in rich colours and beautiful shapes, and, most important, in gold. Gilt knobs, gilt handles and gilt tassels, turned a place of entertainment into a palace. The fairground contained many palaces and each one was a wild experience.

The roundabout of that period was certainly a palace. It combined grace with beauty and all were attracted to it. Since that time, as with many things, grace has given way to noise, loud noise which deafens and at the same time destroys more intimate sounds. The roundabout had charm. It revolved at no great speed, as the alternate horses or cockerels slid gracefully up and down on their twisted brass guides. Some of the ladies astride their horses, looked as if they were off for a morning ride, then presumably, back to the palace. The centre portion of the roundabout in the light of many bulbs, looked like a baroque monument in an Austrian church, except that as the outer part revolved with its riders, various bits of the ornament moved as the music was produced. The helter-skelter was exciting, the swings were dangerous, the dodgem cars were tremendous – except for the silly people who jammed others at the edge – but the roundabout, with all its grace, was to me, the fairground.

"**Le's zee if I can knock 'ee down a coconut,**" slurred my father. The man handed him a number of balls for his penny, and he threw them all, very hard, hitting the canvas behind, but having no effect on the coconuts. "**Buggers be ztuck on,**" he complained, "**le's zee if we can vind the beer tent.**" As he had just come from there, which accounted for his bad shots, it is no wonder my mother said: "**'Tis time we were gwoen hwome.**" He appeared not to hear her, which pleased me a great deal. However, a "**nice young man**" aimed at a coconut, at first go knocked it off, and with a grin, presented it to my mother. The following day my father was offered a piece, which he refused, saying: "**The zhowman unztuck woone vur 'ee did'n?**" My mother, chewing a piece, smiled and nodded.

Flower-shows are for particular people, simply, those who wish to show things. A rather obvious statement made in the cause of those who are not exhibitionists. I knew the people in the village who planned their lives around the show and producing things for it. "**Can't goo on holerday then, 'cos me zweet paes 'll be at their best,**" or "**Dwon't touch they, vur they be vur zhowen.**" I believe all those exhibits looked so unnatural, even the vases of flowers looked unnatural. Just three potatoes in a dish. "What good are three potatoes?" I thought, and wondered what the other six hundredweight were like. About ten gooseberries, big red gooseberries, sitting in a dish.

"So what?" I thought, "we had big gooseberries at home in our garden." I said had, because we did, and they were big. They were delicious too. Iris and Darthy had more than I, taking the view, "**We might as well be hung for a sheep as a lamb.**" My father had found us tucked away behind the bushes, and dragged us away, saying: "**When we d' want y' t' pick 'em an top an' tail 'em y' woon't.**" My mother took over the summary trial, announcing: "**You got noo right t' be there.**" I drew myself up and answered for Darthy, who, in my opinion, had every right to be there. "**But mam, Darthy was born there.**" "**That was another bush altogether,**" said my mother, which left me puzzled. The group of bushes we had semi-stripped were our only gooseberry bushes. "**But mam ...**" Too late, my mother, in one of her determined moods, had taken a basin to rescue those we had left. Better to keep out of the way, otherwise we might have been landed with picking – but no eating. Her remark from the bushes was loud and clear: "**An' dwon't blame me if you get pinches**" [stomach-ache].

No, on consideration our family were not exhibitionists. My father summed it up: "**Vlowers be vur looken at, an' vegetables be vur aten.**" We disagreed greatly, but I saw eye to eye with him on that subject. I thought beyond that and felt of the whole garden and the house, they were for living in and not for show. I do wish my mother had thought the same. "**Dwon't press yer nwose agin the**

winder [window] **pane, what will people think?"** If my father was going out for the evening, he might say: **"Do it matter what they think?"** With the evening at home in prospect, he would have smiled and read the bit of the paper he was reading, again.

The *Western Gazette* came on Friday. The newspaper was popular in the country areas, chiefly for the Situations Vacant columns. When my father had seen them, as he had done for the last ten years, but had not reacted, we might look at the local news. "Flower Show," Prizes were awarded as follows: The list was the same as last year. One or other parent would say: **"'Tis all dizided avore hand."**

"All a matter of luck," some said, while others disagreed, **"Noo zich thing, do all happen if 'ee work vor it."** They argued further, **"Dwon't believe in vate, or in ghwosts, mind 'ee, back last winter ..."** then came the story, the truth of which only its chief character and I knew.

Joe, just to give him a name, walking from the Manor in the dark, **"back last winter,"** was passing the churchyard when he saw a figure in white, **"an eangel,"** he said, above a tombstone. In his own words: **"When I did come near the stwone, the ghwost did disappear, zoo I did run t' the Inn, where I did zhout vor a drink, vor me knees were knocken."** The story passed round the village and as Joe was a genuine sort and not given to wild emotional outbursts, it was accepted as the truth.

It is safe after these years to reveal the facts, and again I remind the reader of the utter truth of each experience in my story. My 'paramour,' if I may be bold enough to call her that? You know the lady in question. She was in her white nightdress just before going to bed, and looking out of her window, across the lawns, over which dancing feet had softly drifted during the day, as had my admiration for her, saw a red glow coming from the church windows. Remembering the church had been gutted by fire early in the century, she ran across the lawn and along the path to the church. Climbing on to a tombstone, she peeped in to see what was happening. The seven red floating lamps along the rood-screen had been replenished that day and were burning rather high, thus casting a red flickering glow within the church. All was well, or was it? At that moment came a man's heavy footsteps along the path, which was Joe approaching the churchyard wall. She, not wanting a man to see her in her night attire, except of course he with whom she shared a marital relationship, darted behind the tombstone, and from Joe's angle, disappeared.

I am glad she told me, and as copyright normally ceases fifty years on, I feel it right others should know. Before that time, it was common to say to a person who looked rather pale: **"You look as if you've zid** [seen] **a ghwost,"** after, as it might have drawn the reply: **"I have,"** the statement fell into disuse. I have often wondered why she told her story to me, and me alone. I believe, because I was special and was trusted not to speak of our secret, and perhaps she thought I was the one person, who at some time in the future would write about it. If that was her thought, you will now have read of an event of some fifty years ago, which is true. An event presented as fact, fact that cannot have been heard or read at any time or place before.

No matter what my academic abilities were, and my thick-headedness in not planning an education on which to build my future, I had great ambition. I had great ambition and at least one smaller ambition. The day arrived for it to be fulfilled, as I waited for the bus to take me to Bournemouth. This was my first trip unaccompanied, and with a fair amount of saving up, my plans had been carefully laid, so that for the first time I could indulge in luxuries. The main aim of my solo trip was to visit a hairdresser – I had learned not to say barber. My first barber was, as you may have guessed, my mother. There was a standing joke in my part of the world: **"Yur hair d' look as if yur mam have done it wi' a pudden basin,"** I laughed with my tormentors, then wiped the laugh from my face, in the pretence of enjoying a joke, for, as again you may have guessed, that is exactly how my hair had been cut. The basin put over my head, then cutting round its edge.

Eventually I became exasperated with the 'manly' boys' remarks and went to the gardener to have my hair cut. he was an excellent gardener and a good barber too. He charged sixpence which was expensive for a non-professional. His wife banished his hairdressing to the stable, because of the mess. **"Dwon't let the birds git hwold of any o' the hair tha's lyen about, or you'll die."** she warned. There was lots of hair strewn on the cobbles outside the stable, yet none of the boys died. For the first time, with hand clippers – not hedge clippers – the hair on the pole of my neck was cut, giving me a sense of well-being and steering me towards being a man. Short back and sides were essential; "A boy," they said, "must look neat about the head, wear a tie and collar under a suit, preferably dark. He must walk with wide steps, and for a period of ten years (7 to 17) he should not play with the girls." Playing before seven was for fun or companionship, and after seventeen, for exactly the same reason – **"wonly different." "Drow yer lag wover,"** [throw your leg over] instructed my father, when I rode his bicycle, **"when you d' git on, or they'll think you'm a 'doman"** [old woman]. That was the propaganda carried from the Victorian era into the nineteen thirties.

On arrival in Bournemouth I went to the Regent Cinema, where, on a balcony, a waiter served me lunch. The sheer extravagance of salad to begin, and served on a half-moon shaped glass dish, was frightening. I held my end up through each course and when finished, dallied, listening to the orchestra before depositing a small tip and leaving. Later I would see the film at the Odeon and have tea on a tray. This was as near to decadence as a village boy dare go.

The hairdresser fiddled and fussed, gushed and gurgled, carrying on an endless conversation – with himself. I was intent on my image in the mirror and acting as if I did this every day. The day had gone according to plan, till as he began dusting me down, he said: "Anything on?" Like a shot I replied: "Not really, just seeing a film and ..." Too late. I overtipped and crept through the wealthy 'with-it' crowds, hoping they would not see my deep-red face.

Shaftesbury

19

A BUS trip to Wimborne on Market Day was a much more homely affair, though, making a detour through the surrounding villages, a rather long-winded journey. **"Hang on a minute, I'll jist goo an' git me chickens,"** said the first lady, as the driver negotiated large boxes of fruit and eggs on to the roof of the bus. The bus, run by a contractor, had a deep guard-rail around its roof and ropes for securing the piles of produce yet to be collected. **"Gi' us a hand wi' these pullets will 'ee,"** said the woman, as she turned to pick up a large basket of flowers, all set into bunches ready for the market stall. The driver, settled in his seat, was detained from starting. **"Jist a mo',"** called the lady from the Post Office, **"Can 'ee take they in vor me?"** as she handed him a pair of shoes. **"Zole an' heel an' I do want 'em be Vriday."** She smiled, waved to the bus in general, then went back to her counter where a little queue had formed.

More frantic waving from a woman at the end of a long path. The driver stopped the bus, sighed and got out, making his way up the winding path. A long conversation followed, which by actions and lip-reading was on these lines: – all his replies were 'yes' or 'no' and were easily 'read' – **"Her lag is it? or is it her arm? They zaid zhe hadden bin well, mystery idden it? Ye', well y' know what they zay, veed a cwold an' ztarve a vever. Tidden a cwold? nur a vever? Ah well, 'tis zummit, I'll be bound. I yerd as how zhe bin t' the doctor, but he coulden do nothen vur her. Never did think much o' doctors. Ah, you tell her t' ate plenty o' onions, that'll put her right."** The driver tried to get away. **"Dwon't vurgit now will 'ee?"** He hurried down the path. **"Vind out the price o' tiddies** [potatoes] **will 'ee an' let I know when 'ee d' come back."** He nodded, not looking at her, but searching for the latch of the gate. **"I'll have a cup o' tae vur 'ee, when 'ee d' call."** She waved as the bus roared off up the hill, the driver, even viewed from the rear, a model of patience.

So the journey continued, with all its intimate conversations. The modern bus operator might say, **"What a way to run a business?"** Oddly, it was the way, and it does my heart good to know that operators are running **"round the village"** services again. I enjoyed the trip to Wimborne, but as the return trip took even longer, I came back by pony and trap. The slow trot-trot was much quicker than returning by the bus. Market ladies always have plenty to talk about, and after a couple of glasses of stout, there was much good-humoured banter each time the bus stopped to let a be-parcelled lady off. Time was found to bring a conversation to a satisfactory conclusion. Sitting alongside the farmer on the driving seat of the trap, one needed only two bits of conversation. **"Things beant what they used t' be,"** and **"No"** [said with a sigh]. These could be fitted to any situation. A passing pretty girl, a field of corn, a new sports car, or the lack of high hedges, behind which the farmer could 'goo': **"My word, I do need t' goo,"** he complained, **"An' things o' nature must be attended to."**

"Can't beat the wold-vashioned things," the farmer said, but his remark was ignored by my parents. Gran had died, quite suddenly and peacefully. One moment she was there with her smile, her reassurance and her farthings for sweets and the next she was gone. It was not going to her little house that hurt most. The long garden, the double gates and the stile into the field, all went with her. Standing by the bonfire with her precious things going up in smoke, hurt even more. The sideboard, the table and its red tasselled cloth, the little side tables with twisted legs and three little brass-clawed feet, and, worst of all, the pictures, which she would look upon and sigh over no more. There was soon to be a new sideboard at home. Gran had left a little money, but spending it that way, while her Victorian sideboard, with its shelves, mirrors and glass front, had been destroyed, seemed to be very near to sacrilege.

Gran might have said: **"Do 'ee kip me zidebwoard vur it be zolid mehogany,"** and she might have added: **"Wi' the money, goo an' git theezelf a ton o' coal."** Our supply of coal was two hundredweights a week, or sometimes three. **"'Nother hunderd this wick,"** my mother might call, waiting to hear the three thuds before producing the money. There was always somewhere near a ton in the coal house, but that was in reserve. There was a large reserve of most household items, and an additional special reserve of many things. **"You never knoow."** she would say, **"There mid** [might] **be a rainy day."** From a cursory inspection there might have been forty days and forty nights of rain in store, with no Mount Ararat in sight when the flood subsided. Part of the 'reserve, reserve,' was a pile of cinders. Each day the ashes would be sifted and the cinders reserved for banking up a coal fire. The ashes made a large heap in the garden ready for spreading. **"Do kip they zlugs away vrom the zweet paes, an' do help the groun'."** said my father.

Without an orchestra to play *Hearts and Flowers,* I have to record that they were hard times and economies were essential. My father did all our boot and shoe repairs. As with decorating, he knew 'the trade,' in this case the harness-maker; so leather and tacks were very cheap, if at any cost at all to him. Sitting on the shed floor with a last and several little piles of leather, and with the aid of one sharp knife, he carved another sole or heel. With his lips holding a good number of tacks he could 'snob' and talk at the same time. With a **"Dwon't zcuff they out z' quick,"** he began another pair.

Using the dialect he might say: **"Thick bwoat do let water in."** Out of context one needed to be careful, for bwoat can be boot or boat. Confusion with the dialect sometimes arose and in a poem I show some of that confusion.

Misunderztanden Ztan

Wold Joe did goo t' have a drink,
  Vur Ztan, 'ee never ardered narn,
"Ztan idden comen I dwon't think,"
  Zaid Joe, "'Ee's cutten o' his carn."
"'Ee's never cutten carn t'day,
  Thee must'a bin mistook in it,"
Tha's what all t'other vo'ks did zay
  "Z' terr'ble wet his vit'll git."
"Wold Ztan," zaid Joe, "Looked at his vit,
  An' zaid as how 'ee thought 'twould rean,
Ah, zwore 'twere time vur cutten it –
  That is, vur cutten it agean."
The vo'ks zaid, "Hwoly Zeants alive,
  Wold Jozeph, thee dost goo too vur,

Noo varmer ever took a zive
    T' cut his carn – not twice a yer."
"Vour times," zaid Joe, "Vour times – well 'bout,
    An' mwore, if it d' grow agean,
Vour times, 'ee teakes his reazor out,
    'Twere vive las' yer, each time did rean."
The vo'ks did laugh: "A reazor Joe?
    A reazor vur t' cut his carn?
Cut ztalk be ztalk, but not too low,
    Carred yer be yer, back t' the barn?"
"Jist roun' the edge the reazor gooes,
    Wold Ztan d' knoow what 'ee's about,
He'm careful not to cut his tooes,
    Then, be the roots, 'ee pulls it out."
Wold Ztan did jine 'em vur zome beer,
    But thought it ztreange when 'ee did come,
Vur t'others, zhowen o' zome vear,
    All zimmed t' be a'gooen hwome.

Corn-cutting time (that in the field) was perhaps the happiest of my childhood. Taking my father's tea across the stubble fields, till I found him, and waiting for his comment: **"I zhan't ate all that."** Tea in the cornfield is a happy memory, and in the setting-sun glow of the evening, the long trek home, where I may have been grumbled at for not wearing old shoes. The stubble was unkind to shoes and helped to wear them out. Iris wore her shoes out while skipping. It is a wonder she did not wear her tongue out, for in those marathons of skipping the rhythm of the patter needed to match the constant swing of the rope. However one got used to that, as to the ticking of a clock. My mother so often said: **"As long as 'ee can yer** [hear] **kids, they be all right, 'tis when they d' goo quiet 'tis worryen."** When I was quiet, it meant I was up a tall tree – to get away from the rotten skipping – where I had scraped my boots going up, though most of the damage to boots and trousers, was in my coming down again. Darthy's shoes were worn out in dancing, not the country dancing I had done, but modern dancing. It *would* be after my first two years at school that my blue-eyed choreographer allowed the pupils to learn pop music and songs for dancing to, and for their stepping out into the world. Just think, I might have held her close – as I did in the dance hall later – instead of at the sedate arm's length of the *Butterfly*.

Darthy danced as some smoke, drink, or take drugs. She aimed to be a proper dancer, though failing in her ambition. She did sing as well as dance and later, with a friend who played the piano accordian, she toured with an amateur dance band. I hesitate to use the word 'hostess,' but she did demonstrate and remonstrate on the dance floor. I envied her her tango, but not the bony figure she developed from constant movement and dashing to and fro without proper meals.

Dancing with my Shadow, we sang, and they danced on in the village hall. That was Saturday, but Sunday brought the *News of the World* and on its front page appeared a large cartoon. That Sunday the cartoonist had chosen Hitler – some sinister character we knew little about, but soon would – as his subject. His caption stuck in my mind, as I remember the shadow of the Dictator falling across a city: **"Danzig with my Shadow."** Who cared about all that. **"Churchill be a warmonger,"** said my mother, and **"There woon't be another war like the last woone,"** added my father. The singing and dancing continued. *On the Isle of Capri, Red Sails in the Sunset,* and numerous sad and sentimental ballads. It is interesting to note, though the songs were simple, their melodies were hummed, sung or whistled by children and older people alike.

Many of us looking back, have said, we lived in the Silly Thirties, yet there was much freedom, laughter and fun in the air. Cornflakes took the place of porridge and ovaltine of cocoa. I welcomed both with open mouth. Friday was still fish day, and Good Friday a very special day.

"Dwon't 'ee bang a nail in, whatever 'ee d' do," my mother warned on Good Friday. The villagers, closely bound to the church were unlikely to do so. Devout people spent three hours in church, those who felt they ought, spent two, and those who 'bent in that direction' spent only one hour. Those who did not attend, were expected to be suitably sombre in their homes. No digging in the garden, because of the use of a sharp instrument, in fact no unnecessary work at all. We had sung sad hymns for forty days and I suspect most of the children did not get the proper sense of "There is a green hill far away, *without* a city wall." We certainly thought the hill had no wall, but later we were taught the true meaning. I knew then, as I know now, that to change that word to 'outside' would ruin the verse. No swearing, no pop music and not too much shouting, was the order of Good Friday. We were devout Anglicans, even though some did not 'bow and scrape' much. I cannot imagine hearing in the village, the conversation I heard a few years later in a London cafe:

Proprietor: Would you like a hot cross bun?
Customer: Christ no!

I might almost have heard, early on Good Friday morning in my village:

Hot cross buns, hot cross buns,
One a penny, two a penny,
Hot cross buns.

Early that morning the baker came with the buns, still hot from the bakery, which made the day rather special. Easter Sunday followed with its flowers, often its sunshine and the 'newness' of spring. Easter meant to us that life began again. Our lives, though poor, were dedicated to the country around us, where life was renewed.

The Easter holiday had not yet arrived, and there were more 'little' exams to be done at school. Who was the son of King So and So? I was asked. I might as well have answered: "Thing-a-me-bob," because I got it wrong. My interest was in the infants' singing next door, the piano strumming, rather than playing. The singing stopped and line by line, following their teacher, came: surely the worst rhyming couplet on record:

Goosey goosey gander,
Where do you wander, ...?

Even as an infant I felt one or other word needed altering or mis-pronouncing, making gander, gaunder, or change wander to meander. Whilst the Kings and

Queens of England and/or Scotland were being put in their correct places by my loyal class-mates – that is loyal to Crown and Head – I was thinking on the words from next door:

> The north wind doth blow and we shall have snow,
> What will poor robin do then, poor thing?
> He'll sit in the barn, to keep himself warm ....

Barn – warm, you see what I mean! **"Too many brandies lead to assault on woman."** said my father. **"Drink be evil,"** answered mam, **"'Tis the downvall o' z' many,** she went on. My mother **"went on"** about a lot of things, but as many of us, she went on about things she perhaps felt a little sympathy for. My father was reading the *News of the World,* the Sunday 'read' for so many. A little entertainment between two heavy weeks, in which they had little time to read, let alone consider vice. **"Terr'ble,"** said my father, **"What is?"** answered my mother, peeling potatoes, then, **"Read it to me,"** she added, paring more furiously. **"The young woman was assaulted in the flat while her husband slept. In the early hours of Thursday morning, a man entered the flat, and throwing the woman on to a bed, said ...."** **"Jist a minute,"** my mother chipped in, **"Goo on out t' play you childern."** **"Oh mam,"** we complained, **"Why?"** my mother, busy wiping her hands and hushing my father, continued **"Because,"** and out we went. Sex, that is what it was, as evil as drink? Moderation seemed to be the deciding factor.

Had I known the word moderation and acted upon it, my crisis may not have arisen. It was cider-making time, and cart-loads of apples had been placed in the cart shed, ready for making into cider. Next door stood a huge press and its rough timbers carried a long shaft for turning the tall spindle, which in turn lowered a huge square block of wood. In the big square tray below, was placed a layer of straw, on which, having passed through the mangle, a large amount of apples, now in pulp form, was spread. The operation continued until it was a five-tiered 'sandwich,' then the turning and pressing began.

If any of my readers saw the film *Alf's Button Afloat,* which was showing then, there is a scene, where the button is rubbed – originally part of the magic lamp – and the Genie appears. **"What is your wish, oh Master?"** Together they wished for 'beer,' but the Genie got it wrong and produced a bier. They were shocked and very quickly explained the difference. Then it happened, there they were with barrels of beer and all was perfect bliss. I tell you this, because one character, flat on his back, with his mouth under a barrel's tap, wore a look of complete ecstasy. That was me under the cider-press. With a straw, corn straw, there I lay; oblivious of time or place.

"Wha's the matter wi' you?" my father enquired, **"This be the fifth time t'night you bin up."** **"Got the runs, dad,"** I replied – running. **"Bin aten apples I 'zpose?"** **"No dad,"** I said meekly, but he knew. **"Wha's the matter wi'n,"** called my yawning mam, **"Bin drinken,"** smiled my father. **"Dwon't be daft,"** scoffed my mother, **"Now goo on back t' bed, 'tis wonly dree [three] "o'clock."**

20

I SUSPECT even the Archbishop of Canterbury has wicked thoughts, and because of that I need not have felt too guilty about my own, when, as a child, boredom set in. I confess a number of them, perhaps to rid myself of a little guilt. I often thought of people in the most unlikely places. The King in the lavatory, with the Queen smiling, but shouting at him to hurry up, as the coach was waiting. The Prime Minister, Neville Chamberlain, in his pin-striped suit and with his rolled umbrella, digging up lots of potatoes, and leaving them to dry, while he milked thirty cows, then with an aching back, picking up the potatoes. None of these mental pictures fitted. Worse, were my thoughts which strayed in, of all places, church.

Like laughter, once thoughts bubble up, they are difficult to suppress. My act of worship sometimes proceeded on these lines: "I believe in God the Father, Almighty, Maker of heaven and earth, and .... I wonder if Mr and Mrs So and So, when they go to bed and take off all their clothes, those furs, coats and things, are they the same as others underneath all that? Do they chase each other round the room, surely not? Do they tickle each other? and do they laugh? I had never seen them laugh. Or do they ......? and if they do .... and ... and ..., where was I? .. and ... and the life everlasting. Amen."

"I must ask my Lord's forgiveness," I thought. I saw him often in church, normally up in the gallery near the organ, but it would be difficult to approach him there. I rarely saw him down with the ordinary folk. He may have felt his voice carried better from there, and I feel sure he was right. You see he had sworn at me, called me everything – and more. From him I had not expected that, but no doubt I had asked for it. I would try to see him when he appeared at the gate to the churchyard, and I would say: "My Lord," I suppose I had to begin that way? "My Lord," I would say, "I humbly beseech," no, there was no need to be humble. "My Lord, I am most deeply sorry I incurred your wrath," but it sounded wrong. "My Lord," but his manservant said, "Me Lord." Perhaps I should ignore the title and come straight to the point: **"Last Saturday mornen you were hunten on Harley Down,** [I could slip in a 'Me Lord', there] **and the hounds were chasen the fox, with you an' all the hosses behind them. I saw the fox, and wanten to be helpful, I stood in its way, till it went in another direction. That is when** [Me Lord] **you swore at me.** [Might I add?] **Even as Lord of the Manor, you shouldn't do that, not use words that even my father didn't use."** Anyway I did not ask his forgiveness, because I was glad the fox got away.

"Come next Quarter Day, we mid be out o' house an' hwome," said my father, indicating I should know better. Better? I did not know what a Quarter Day was, I only had a vague idea. Those who dealt with legal matters knew, as did all the tenants in the village, whether farmer or cottager, that rents were due on each Quarter Day. As the Lord of the Manor owned everything in sight, and many villages beyond that, it was best as a tenant, not to forget the Quarter Days. The 25th March, Lady Day (The Virgin Mary), the 24th June, Midsummer Day, the 29th September, Michaelmas Day, (St Michael) and Christmas Day. The one most used for transfer of job/cottage, was Michaelmas. I always thought it sad that Christmas Day should be a Quarter Day, that being the day one could be **"turned out o' house an' hwome."**

"**I can always git a job,**" said my father and that was true, he was good at many jobs. His woodwork skills were never passed on to me, but I inherited a little of the art of upholstering. If we needed a new piece of furniture, finances often would not allow it, so off went my father to the saleroom at Blandford "**Vur jist what we do want.**" His first pleasure was in the bidding, then in an onlooker's remark: "**My word, you got thick chest o' drawers cheap, but they'm wonly deal.**" By the time my father had finished they were "**zolid woak,**" and my mother accepted them with pride. He would have stripped old paint or varnish from the deal, and applied an undercoat of cream paint. This was followed by the real artistry. He put in the grain, by 'dragging' the stain in a certain way. Many front doors were done in the same way by professionals. He did not waste his time in mixing with them, picking up their knowledge – and the odd tin of varnish.

My father aimed at obtaining 'gratis,' but my mother struck hard bargains, yet that is not quite true, my mother thought she was driving a bargain, especially with door-to-door salemen, who, when they reduced to 'give-away' level, were actually making a handsome profit. The Indian, complete with turban, was at some advantage, as my mother was frightened at the start. His case was open and things on show, when she said "**Dwon't wopen yur cease,**" and the table-cloth in fine silk, resting in her hand before she said: "**I han't got noo money.**" She had lost the battle, because he said: "Pay me when I next see you." Immediately she found the cash, as she had no desire to owe money, or for that matter, to see him again. For thirty years a resident of Birmingham, the Indian knew his business and the British housewife.

Gipsies at the door were equally successful. The trouble was they knew the householders, and pretended to be as poor as they. The hard luck story normally worked, and with their knowledge of customers, they told the future from past experience, on the principle of "the more you spend, the better your future," as my poem indicates.

Darzet Gipsy

You've zid a lot a' trouble dear,
I zees it in yur veace,
There's plenty mwore t' come I vear,
Unless thees buy zome leace.
　　Zome pags? ah, it d' teake zome hours
　　T' meake they artivicial vlowers.

Dree dozen? ah, tha's better now,
Yur life line's long an' clear,
You'll zee a hunderd yers I 'llow,
But watch thick line that veer.
　　There's lacks o' money I'll be boun' –
　　Two cards o' buttons, 'alf a crown.

Wide 'lascit, zixpence vur a yard,
I'll cut 'ee off 'bout vour,
Thee's knowed o' times that 'ave bin hard,
But wousn't knoow noo mwore.
    There's tragedy, but not vur thee,
    Nur vur thee clwosest vamily.

Min' I dwon't zee things terr'ble good,
Not roun' the carner yet,
I'd like t' zay as how I could,
Luck's on the way I bet.
    Zoo, buy zome heather – I've a hunch
    'Twill come – a tanner vur a bunch.

Yur trouble zeem t' clear away,
There's vartune in yur eyes,
Zoo, what else will 'ee 'ave t'day?
You'm lucky when you buys.
    Not nothen mwore? then I must zay,
    I do zee zadness on the way.

Cheaper vrom Woolworths? ah, zoo it be,
But thee mid think on this,
They coulden tell 'ee how t' zee
Yur vuture zteate o' bliss.
    You got good vartune comen quick –
    I'll bring 'ee mwore, this time next wick.

I had made my solo visit to Bournemouth, so I was allowed to go almost there again. Just on the edge of the town lived Auntie Vi, with her husband and a great number of sons. I have said a great number, because with an additional two players and my uncle in goal, they *were* the local football team. This to me was strange enough, but there was something stranger. In the hallway of the house stood a cigarette slot–machine. A large cast-iron thing which carried several brands of cigarettes. It all began with having enough smokers in the house to make it a convenience, then all the people around came with their coins for their preferred brand. At last Auntie Vi became just a door-opener and her hall might as well have been part of the street. I do not remember completing a conversation with her, for in the middle the door bell rang and with, **"That blasted mazhine,"** she made her way yet again to the front door. One could hear her as she stumbled along the dark passage to the front of the house: **"I'll git rid o' thick mazhine, I woulden mind, but I'm the wonly woone that dwon't zmwoke."** Then as the bell rang again: **"All right, I'm comen."**

"Yes mam, I'm comen," I cried from the river bank, for that is where a great deal of my life was spent. I had dammed the brook, or so I thought, till a minute later the water surged through again. My trousers were rolled up, but still dirty, as were my feet and shoes, though they were taken off when I began sinking deeper. I grabbed some water cress quickly and pulled a couple of yellow iris. Squelching up the bank and across the cow-trodden field, I reached the fence to: **"Come on then,"** dashing under the barbed wire, calling, **"Comen, comen – oh blast,"** as I extended the rent in my Saturday shirt. Arriving at the back door, and I knew the pattern: **"Look at the state o' you, you be naughty t' – ooh you got zome vlowers vur me, I'll jist goo an' put 'em in a vause** [vase] **an' you put that cress in zome water."**

Next day I went with the boy next door, who was now sixteen, to help him look after the steers on the down, and taking a packed dinner, we lit a bonfire below the down at the edge of the lake. We shared our sandwiches and bottles of tea and to end the meal, shared some chocolate. He was still my hero, because he did grown-up things and did them all so cleverly. It was that, and because I was a boy that led to argument and the fighting of a bitter battle near the turnpike. I lost, but that was of no account. Our personalities had clashed, simply because he was no longer a boy, and I felt lost.

Next Sunday came, with no cutting of walking-sticks or striding up the lane, instead he went walking in another lane arm in arm with **"thick common wench,"** and I could not understand why. **"Up under the hidge** [hedge] **they were,"** said my father. "Perhaps he was picking violets," I thought – I hoped – "and would bring them to my mother as usual." As dusk fell, he did not call across the garden or come to the back door.

The pattern of life is always changing, but sometimes the change is very marked. He cycled off to his work in a paper-mill and I took a bicycle ride over the downs. If I needed to think the downs were the place to do it. High up along the bridle paths I travelled, calling against the noise of the wind, the wind that took with it any bitterness that came with growing up.

Soon I could cycle to Salisbury, where the better cinemas were, avoiding Market-day and the traffic that caused. Salisbury Cathedral needs no advertising by me, but, having grown up with Constable's view in our living-room, (one of my mother's **"real oil peantens")** I was surprised to see the spire for the first time from the other side. The view from the Blandford road, on descending the hill towards the city, is breathtaking. There soars the spire, the city masked by the hills and giving the appearance of a painting, but lighter, more delicate than the work of Constable. My first impression on seeing the spire against a clear blue sky, was, "That is surely made of grey lace, so fine is the tracery." I have mentioned my desire to paint, and had I been able, I would have painted Salisbury Cathedral from 'our side.'

Painting, or for that matter any work done on the village green, was far better than in the high-windowed classroom, though in summer there might be the odd cricket ball to consider as it knocked the paint pot over. The village green was certainly the place from which to paint the church, except for the rotten cricketers who got in the way. By the end of the term I could look across the cricket pitch and say: **"Now has the Victor won."** That, I must explain. Victor was one of the older and tougher boys, a good cricketer, with bowling as his speciality. I believe the Head was a little jealous of Victor, who was, more or less a man, and could not be talked down to. The Head treated him badly in class, and Victor, a popular boy, did not take it lightly.

"I'll get him one day," threatened Victor. "How?" I wondered, but was soon enlightened. "I'll bowl and bowl until I get him," said Victor. He bowled dinner hour after dinner hour, day after day, week after week and on any cricket day in between. He bowled constantly – for the Head's legs. I knew and was frightened, the school knew and was frightened too, but fascinated by Victor's determination. The Head knew, but showed no fear; he dare not, nor dare he lose interest in the game, so stood there match after match till Victor 'got him.' Victor spent the rest of his time at school as a hero. The crippled Head was my first living example of vengeance planned and so grimly carried out.

I envied Victor his admirers, more, I envied him his bravery. Surely justice was done? Did the Head not marry my blue-eyed choreographer? true it was before I was born, but I cannot be blamed for that. His loud infectious laugh, heard around the school and across the cool lawns of his garden, was reason enough for injuring him. On the whole cricket, apart from batting, bored me, but that LBW was something I would like to have seen and shouted loudly for: "Howzat?"

Perhaps I was wrong to hold a grudge, but held none against animals. In corners of fields around the village, traps were set for vermin. Gin-traps, set under wooden arched tunnels, were laid to catch stoats or weasels. I saw animals caught in these vicious traps, legs torn through, and put them out of their misery. Oh yes, there is cruelty, even in the beauty of the countryside.

Cruelty is relative so it is said. From my point of view it was cruel to keep me in that tall dark Victorian-built school, when I could have been out on the Dorset downs, free, with my own thoughts. To others it would have been cruel not to harness my potential and turn my mind from poetic lines composed out on the hills, to intelligent study. There is no relativity in torture. A little animal left in pain for hours until it bleeds to death is downright cruelty.

It is human to wipe the bad from one's past and, through rose-coloured spectacles, to see only the good. I have taken great care to retrace my steps and 're-enact' some of my childhood in order to write about it. I have picked a bunch of primroses and felt the warmth of sun still upon them. I have held tight in my hand a bunch of deep-blue violets and felt them cool against my cheek and dropped a pebble into the pool by the bridge, watching the water ripple as it did fifty years ago. I have pricked my hands on holly, scratched my fingers on briers and cleaned good Dorset soil from inside my boots. The lanes are not as long, nor are the walls as high, but the pimpernal and the shamrock are the same, if anything can be the same, when not loved by the young admirer.

Over the woodshed of my old home, grew a deep-purple clematis. It used to reflect in the bucket of water from the nearby well, and drew these lines from me:

> Purple you came as last year
> but are you changed
> and am I different now?
> Your same dark hue will come again
> and I shall admire.
> Will you look at me and wonder?

21

IT IS the sound of Dorset that I wish to capture and hold, even though the past must slip away. The burr of the dialect is as much part of my home county as were the **"ztwones in the vield vur grabben."** I beg those who feel as I do, and as I have pleaded before; go out to the country areas with a tape recorder and capture the sound of the old people, because it is with them that a little of the dialect remains. The written word can never convey the 'feel' of the Dorset dialect, besides which it is difficult for an outsider to read.

The nineteen thirties produced much that was good, a great deal coming, via Hollywood, from America. Modern things are all right in their place, as are modern words, but some of those from the USA were not our best imports. I shall not attempt to list the words, but refer to the first of the bunch, it is of course, 'OK.' However, I would like to refer to something which struck me at that time, and that is the similarity of words and sounds with those we used in Dorset. It is easy to see, or hear, from which part of the country the Pilgrim Fathers set out. **Vall** [fall], the autumn, is a good example, but pronunciation is apparent, as in **bedder,** [better], or **budder,** [butter]. Why, I ask, if an American walked into a west country shop and asked: **"Have y' godda half a-pound o' budder?"** would the proprietor be impressed? but if I walked in with the same request, *in exactly the same words,* he might think me a bit **"wold-vashioned."** Is it because – and this was my fear in the thirties – everything from America is good?

The accent of the 'upper class' was one of the worst products of the period, the period of the drawing-room comedy, when Noel Coward became the king of "good English speech." The landed gentry added affectation to good speech, which was called the Oxford – I get your parden – the Auxford accent. The after effects are still with us, but abhored by most. How silly some of those words were: **"We must have the taup of the tree chaupped auff."** That was, **"'Nough t' put a veller off vur a ztart."** The water was sauft, the pigeons in the lauft, the craufter in his crauft, and, not to mention the way they scauffed at our **"hwomely zoun's."** Comediens often drew their material for gags from the accent of 'top drawer' people who 'cracked their jaws.'

Customer: I would like some pepper.
Shopkeeper: Black pepper or white pepper, Madam?
Customer: Don't be silly, I want writing pepper.

William Barnes wrote his poems in normal English and in the Dorset dialect. He often recorded conversations, which is what I set out to do in the following poem; showing the difference between 'educated' speech and the dialect.

Vicar's Calling

'Tis good t' zee 'ee Pa'son Zire,
   Git thee inzide an' out o' cwold;
I vinds I needs a gert big vire –
   Mind, tidden 'cos I'm gitten wold.

Thank you, Samuel, how very nice,
  The wind blows cold, too cold by far,
Warmth is, forgive me, my own vice;
  But, tell me, Samuel, how you are?

I be all right, vit as a vlee,
  Vur that I tell thee I be glad;
'Tweren't always zoo, noo, I tell thee,
  I do convess that I bin bad.

Confession, Samuel, that is good,
  We, all of us, must err and stray;
But, I have never understood
  How old you are, do tell me pray?

I tell 'ee I beant wold at all,
  I zometimes think it dwon't zim real;
Jist ninety dree – tha's come the vall –
  Well, thee't as wold as thees d' veel.

My goodness gracious, oh dear, dear,
  How splendidly you've 'fought the fight,'
You must take care and not, I fear,
  Go wandering out too late at night.

I dos zometimes wi' Vilet like,
  Vive times a wick an' zometimes mwore:
'Er alms'ouse lies at Nether Wyke,
  A widder zhe be – zembty vour.

Good Heavens – forgive me – I must pray
  For you, for Violet, for us all;
I came to give you strength today,
  They said, "He needs you, please do call."

An' thees 'ave called, zoo 'ave noo vear,
  A Pa'son gen'lly underztan's,
We've called vur presents, vlowers an' beer –
  Now we wants thee t' call the banns.

I never heard a voice raised in objection when banns were called, but I heard voices during Harvest Festival. Harvest was the busiest time for all those who worked on farms, and when it was all over the women and children busied themselves in decorating the church. The whole building was transformed, as if it were a garden, so that the beauty of nature linked with that of the church. After Harvest Festival the flowers were given to the Cottage Hospital and the produce to the elderly of the village. Towards the back of the church one heard them whispering: **"I could do wi' the tiddies, [potatoes] but I dwon't want the** zwedes." or: **"Tell 'ee what, I woulden mind a couple pots o' that honey, but I dwon't want the jam, 'cos I did gi' that mezelf."**

We plough the fields and scatter the good seed on the land ...

"Last yer they didden bring me noo aggs, zoo I zhall ask vur zome."

All good gifts around us are sent from heaven above ...

"Noo use dependen on 'eaven, I zhall tell 'em what I d' want."

Voilent **"shushes"** from most of the congregation. **"Got yer penny vur collection?** was followed by a searching, finding, losing and finding again. More loud whispers: **"I've lost me place,"** followed by more **"shushes,"** and so the service continued to *Praise the Song of Harvest Home.* Hardly had "peace ... be with you this night and for evermore," been uttered, than the remarks of the old folk became louder: **"I dwon't knoow about 'arvest Hwome, but tha's where I be a-gwoen; do git cwold in October."** Then from at least one of them as a parting shot: **"Dwon't vurgit t' put I in zome honey, but I dwon't want any o' they parznips, vur they d' gi' I indigestion, ah, that they do."**

Perhaps some visitors enjoyed the evening service earlier in the summer, without all the vegetables and additional chants. Weary, after touring around the county, they may have found the peace I knew there. With the West door open and the glow from the sunset streaming through, picking out the colours and glinting on the gold of its decoration, they might have lingered to hear: "…. until the shades lengthen and the evening comes, and the busy world is hushed, and the fever of life is over, and our work is done ..." before departing, perhaps the richer for their visit.

They, with a few men from the congregation, might have gone to the next village, because our pub was not open on Sundays. To have it open would indeed have been wicked, the idea descending as a rigid rule from the past, to keep the working classes away from temptation. Even during the week drinking had to be accompanied by proper conduct. Men in the public bar, ladies in the 'Ladies Room,' that is those who cared about their reputation. Those who did not, and in that respect my mother was included, went to the Jug and Bottle panel – to see into and be seen by, the public bar – where they tapped gently for service: **"Zmall glass o' ztout please, dree bottles o' lemonade an' dree bags o' chips** [crisps] **vur the nippers"** [outside playing in the garden].

I have described our bungalow as being a peaceful place, which it was, but with certain reservations. All was calm, when suddenly my mother jumped up and ran into the garden. Breathless, she came back, to our enquiring: **"What on earth's the matter?"** **"Jist bin t' zee the new moon,"** she gasped, **"Musten zee'n drough** [through] **winder"** [window]. Up and off again, this time to the bedroom, and coming back: **"Jist bin t' turn me money"** [at new moon], then settled for a moment. **"Don't move,"** we might say, as we tried to catch a tiny spider. She beat us to it, but to the rescue, and, winding it in her hair, proclaimed: **"He'll bring me money"** [the small spider was called a money spider]. Besides being superstitious, my mother had tremendous faith. Relaxed for a moment, then up again because someone had spilled some salt. Carefully she picked it up, throwing some over her left shoulder three times, just to make sure no bad luck would come about. No use, under any circumstances, asking my mother "Could you pass the salt please?" She would shake her head grimly, saying: **"Help 'ee t' zalt, help 'ee t' zorrow."**

Then, sitting at peace by the fire, she was up, as if spotting a cobra about to strike. **"Look, ooh, dear, dear, dear, I'll zoon git that out o' it."** She had found a small piece of elder wood among the firewood by the grate. Picking it up as if it contained some magic, or would infect the bearer, she carried it into the garden, throwing it far into the bushes. Coming back to settle, she said: **"Mid as well have the devil in house, as elder."** We all sighed and relaxed once more, apart from Darthy, who was cleaning her shoes. A yell from my mother: **"Teake thick zhoe off o' teable, 'tis terr'ble bad luck."** A grunt from Darthy, who went off to the back shed where there was an old table, on which to do odd jobs. My mother often came from there with the wood chopper in her hand – she is going to murder father, we feared – shouting: **"Dwon't 'ee ever leave a hook on teable, that be wuss** [worse] **luck than any o' it."**

It is a wonder any of the family lived for long, indeed I wonder I am here to tell of the dire things that should have occurred. If sheets were folded and creased in the middle, and there appeared the shape of a coffin, it was, **"A zure zign o' deaf** [death] **in the vam'ly."** With our walls covered with pictures, one was bound to fall now and again. **"Zomebody in the vam'ly will die."** Escaping death did not mean freedom from disaster. Two knives crossed on the table meant a fight and stepping on a beetle made it rain. To me it seemed a vast jungle of taboos, and if I escaped one, the other waited to ensnare me.

Just as our minds were cluttered with all the omens of **"Bad vartune,"** so was the house, inside and out, cluttered with the symbols of good luck. Stones with holes in, hung on every possible projection, horse shoes, positioned *the right way up,* or one heard: **"Come quick, a zhoe be valled down,"** and bits of coal, which were on no account, for burning. Add to this the number of wishbones and numerous pieces of heather – from the gipsies – which were to be found in vases, tins and yes, there was even heather in a wardrobe, but that should not have been confused with lavender, which was there to deter moths. Perhaps the heather kept at bay the bad luck of having the woollens eaten through by moths? **"Dwon't turn 'em right way round,"** my mother insisted. Someone had put a garment on inside out, **"Or you'll zpoil yur luck."** The unfortunate – fortunate? – individual went through the day in great discomfort. Underpants are not at their best inside out.

Mam was little better outside the house. Out for a stroll and suddenly breaking into a run, meant she had heard the cuckoo for the first time, or any bird may have dropped its lime on a pure white sheet, which was hanging on the clothes line, airing after ironing. **"Dwon't teake it off, vur tha's yur luck."** So, we went back indoors to relax with a cup of tea, and, as luck would have it, there was a circle of froth on mine: **"'Tis yur luck, 'tis the zize o' a zhillen, ah, you be comen int'a zome money."** I felt I was unlucky being surrounded by so much luck, good or not; restricting it certainly was.

"If I be lucky," said my father, **"I zhall git thick bunch o' tools, when I do bid."** The tools were one lot from the sale of all the farm machinery and implements. The tenants were moving on, and with them their daughter Peggy. Peggy, with the dark fringed hair and red full lips, Peggy, with whom I had danced in the country dances and shared sweets, Peggy who had played the Mayor and I the Piper in the *Pied Piper of Hamelin,* I the piper who could not rid our back chalk wall of a few rats, let alone Hamelin of a plague.

Me: If I rid your town of rats, will you give me a thousand guilders?
He [she]: A thousand, we will give you fifty thousand.

[The piper steps out into the street, blows one shrill blast on his pipe and all the rats follow him to the river and drown.]

The story as you know, continues with the Mayor refusing to pay the Piper – having called the tune – so the Piper entices all the children away. The trouble was, my rats and children were all the same, except some were on all fours. Had I been a genuine 'whistler-up' of rats, I might have enticed some from our back wall, across our little stage and down to the river. Peggy, with her dark hair and red lips, which matched her dressing gown, trimmed with cotton wool for ermine, took her last bow that day and by the end of it was gone. "Why don't things stay the same?" I thought.

Among my collection of cigarette cards was a set showing racing cars. Those sleek models, one of which I longed to drive, brought much fascination to small boys, perhaps because they were similar to the sports cars we saw on the turnpike each Sunday. **"This one goes sixty miles an hour,"** we gasped, as our parents shook their heads, saying: **"Never zhould be 'llowed."** The fastest on land, the fastest on water, the fastest in the air and of course, churning the mud along our country lanes, the fastest tanks from Salisbury Plain. All those young men who wanted to be soldiers, young men bringing our forces into the fast machine age. They had already made familiar to us the bren gun carrier, fast on its tracks, and carrying a rapid and accurate weapon of war. Those were some of the things that troubled parents with young sons, during the night, and bothered some young people during the cloudy days.

"Dwon't think about it," said my father, **"There woon't be nar war, the last woone were a war t' end all wars."** In the dialect war has the same sound as car. Sports Day came and my mother hobbled in a sack to win the parents' race. She did it with a foot through one corner of the sack. She was disqualified from the egg and spoon, because, although first past the tape, she held the egg in position with her other hand. I feel sure her motto was **"If it can't be done be zkill, then meake it easier vur the like o' me."** I won no medals and I certainly did not bob for apples. If I had a motto, it must have been: "People expect so much from winners." The rambler roses were their usual rich reds and pinks, the potatoes were as new and delicious as ever and the cottage loaf I brought home, still hot under my arm, brought the reprimand: **"You bin at'n agean."** Of broad beans I said, and still say: **"I could enjay a dish o' they, hot or cwold, anytime o' day or night."** The sun shone on the white front step, forcing me to shield my eyes to see the pink shamrock, open and surely, smiling. The sun shone everywhere – but on the front-room silk cushions.

The apples were ripening in the orchard and I had grown up enough to wait, but took one, just one, to keep the taste in my mind. The silence in the orchard was church-like and I thought of a poet from the next village who, imagining she was talking to God about life, wrote:

"Under thick there wold apple tree,
Where I do zit an' talk wi' He."

I thought too of our dialect poet William Barnes and his Orcha'd in Linden Lea:

"An' there vor me the apple tree
Do lean down low in Linden Lea."

The songs of the day were sad, so one wondered if the composers felt that way. *When the Poppies Bloom Again,* the sombre sound of the words "The leaves so brown came tumbling down, remember, that September," and the plaintive *When I dream of San Marino.* Oh those songs, and a thousand soldiers' voices singing in a great marquee just beyond the village. I wondered, were their parents thinking of them? or were they indulging in wishful thinking, like mine: **"There woon't be nar war, an' if there is, there woon't be noo trenches, not like the last woone."?**

The summer of 1939 drew to a close and the summer camp with it. With a section of the drum and fife band from Tidworth Tattoo, the regiments paraded and gave a brilliant display in one of the larger fields. The band played a poignant tune and I remembered the words from my infants' class:

"Oh dilly, dilly, dilly, dilly,
Come and be killed ...."

The Lord of the Manor took the salute and spoke in praise of the soldiers of Southern Command. Our priest, who acted as chaplain to the soldiers, stood smiling by one of the tents to be photographed by his daughter. Standing close to 'Monty,' he smiled again and the result was a picture showing happiness. Those two figures looked so tiny among the might of Southern Command, but to me they were War and Peace. Peace I knew, he had trained me in the ways of God; the ways of the world were soon to be made known to me.

I heard the last Last Post from the camp, and the next day the soldiers moved back to the Plain. I also heard an old man of the village say: **"All they young men .....,"** as the angelus rang from the church tower to commemorate those who fell in the Great War. Soon the words of Neville Chamberlain, "... I have to tell you now that no such undertaking has been received, and ..." All of us who had pretended stopped pretending, and said with many across the country:

"'Twill be wover be Christmas."

Equal, those words, across the land and equally wrong. There was peace in the fields and lanes around the village, not even broken by the church bells. They were silenced, only to be used in the event of an invasion.

Thick village o' mine, the vo'k, Dorset, nur me Country, 'ould ever be quite the zeame agean.

Fontmell Magna: still with its maypole

Stour Provost

**The illustrations are by Joseph Pennell,
from Sir Frederick Treves's 'Highways and
Byways in Dorset', 1906.**